FINAL BOARDING CALL

SATAN'S PLAN FOR THE AGES AND OUR LAST MISSION

BY

REV. MATTHEW PATRICK WINFREY

XULON PRESS

FINAL BOARDING CALL
Satan's Plan for the Ages & Our Last Mission
by Rev. Matthew Patrick Winfrey

Printed in the United States of America

ISBN 9781628391367

www.xulonpress.com

ACKNOWLEDGEMENTS

I would like to thank the Lord, for His Grace without which I am totally unable to do anything that is worth doing. Outside of His steadfast love, I am tossed, like a wave in ocean! But He keeps lifting me to do His will!

I wish to especially thank my wife, Jessa, for her encouragement and patience to deal with the missionary/pastor's life, which is a life of sacrifice and faith.

To Rosemary Kelley, who edited this book, and more importantly, helped me get started writing (which I had delayed for a long time). Only the Lord can give friends like her.

To Andrew Kelsall of "ANDREWKELSALL.COM On Line Graphic Design Service" who volunteered his time and design talent to create the cover art for this book: Thank you!

To all the donors of Joshua's Ministry and subscribers of our YouTube channel: We love you! Your prayers and encouragement made this fruit of the ministry possible!

Thank you all and I will love you all eternally!

Your Brother in Christ,

Patrick Winfrey

TABLE OF CONTENTS

Warnings

WARNING:

If you desire to continue to sleep in a lukewarm, touchy-feely "relevant" church or live in the matrix of the lies of this world, stop reading now!

WARNING:

If you want to remain bound by spiritual strong holds and vain imaginations, stop reading now!

WARNING:

If you do not wish to be set on Fire by the Holiness of the Lord's presence, stop reading now!

WARNING:

If you do not desire the Lord to move on your behalf as you begin to *hunger and thirst* after His righteousness, stop reading now!

WARNING:

If you do not want an encounter with Jesus that will turn your life upside down, cleanse you, rebuild you, and change your curses into blessings, stop reading now!

Still reading?

Okay, Here We Go!

INTRODUCTION

The Lord Jesus Christ tells us in Luke 21:24 that one of the signs of His return is that "the times of the Gentiles [would] be fulfilled." St. Paul explains it like this, **"For I would not, brethren, that ye should be ignorant of this mystery, lest ye should be wise in your own conceits; that blindness in part is happened to Israel, until the fullness of the Gentiles be come in." Romans 11:25** Most Bible scholars agree that this refers to the last Gentile to become part of the Church; and that once full, at a number only the Lord knows, the Church of Jesus Christ will be caught up to be with our Bridegroom, as His bride, for eternity. **1 Thessalonians 4:16-18, "For the Lord himself shall descend from heaven with a shout, with the voice of the archangel, and with the trump of God: and the dead in Christ shall rise first: Then we which are alive and remain shall be caught up together with them in the clouds, to meet the Lord in the air: and so shall we ever be with the Lord. Wherefore comfort one another with these words."**

Matthew 24:3-14 is one of the most familiar passages of scripture about the signs of the Second Coming of Christ, **"And as he sat upon the mount of Olives, the disciples came unto him privately, saying, Tell us, when shall these things** be? and what shall be the sign of thy coming, and of the end of the world? And Jesus answered and said unto them, Take heed that no man deceive you. For many shall come in my name, saying, I am Christ; and shall deceive many. And ye shall hear of wars and rumours of wars: see that ye be not troubled: for all these things must come to pass, but the end is not yet. For nation shall rise against nation, and kingdom against kingdom: and there shall be famines, and pestilences, and earthquakes, in divers places. All these are the beginning of sorrows. Then shall they deliver you up to be afflicted, and shall kill you: and ye shall be hated of all nations for my name's sake. And then shall many be offended, and shall betray one another, and shall hate one another. And many false prophets shall rise, and shall deceive many. And because iniquity shall abound, the love of many shall wax cold. But he that shall endure unto the end, the same shall be saved. And this gospel of the kingdom shall be preached in all the world for a witness unto all nations; and then shall the end come."

But, all these signs, do *not* point to the Rapture of the Church, for this is an event that will happen in a moment, in the twinkling of an eye when the Church is suddenly removed from the earth. **1 Corinthians 15:51, "Behold, I shew you a mystery; We shall not all sleep, but we shall all be changed, In a moment, in the twinkling of an eye, at the last trump: for the trumpet shall sound, and the dead shall be raised incorruptible, and we shall be changed."**

Jesus will come for His Bride like a thief in the night, **Matthew 24:43-44, "But know this, that if the goodman of the house had known in what watch the thief would come, he would** have watched, and would not have suffered his house to be broken up. Therefore be ye also ready: for in such an hour as ye think not the Son of man cometh."

This event, the catching away of the Bride of Christ, is generally called the Rapture because the Latin word for being "caught up suddenly" used in 1 Thessalonians. 4:16 is "rapiemur" from which we get the English transliteration, Rapture. (Latin Vulgate of 382 AD: *"Deinde nos, qui vivimus, qui relinquimur, simul rapiemur cum illis in nubibus obviam Christo in aera, et sic semper cum Domino erimus"*)

There is debate over the rapture, which we will not address in this book. But, we are completely convinced that the Rapture is clearly seen in the Bible, and will occur just prior to the Tribulation period of seven years, when the infamous Anti-Christ will rule the earth. This seven year period will commence soon after the sudden catching away of the Church. The Antichrist will come forward, in the midst of the chaos of the rapture, and bring a peace to the while world (Daniel 9:27). The Bible tells us the whole world shall wonder after the Beast / Anti-Christ (Rev 13:3).

The entire period is known by several names, one is "The Day of the Lord." The Rapture is just the opening act of the drama of that Day. The Day will end with His returning and judging those who remain on the earth who have survived The terrible events of the Tribulation period. **Matthew 25:31-34, "When the Son of man shall come in his glory, and all the holy angels with him, then shall he sit upon the throne of his glory:[32] And before him shall be gathered all nations: and he shall separate them one from another, as a shepherd divideth his sheep from the goats:[33] And he shall set the**

sheep on his right hand, but the goats on the left.[34] **Then shall the King say unto them on his right hand, Come, ye blessed of my Father, inherit the kingdom prepared for you from the foundation of the world"**

This Day of the Lord includes His rule on earth for 1000 years. Let's look at a few Bible verses to show you what we mean:

As we can see in this text, the Tribulation period is in the mind of the Apostle Paul as he writes.

1 Thessalonians 5:2-3, "For yourselves know perfectly that the day of the Lord so cometh as a thief in the night. For when they shall say, Peace and safety; then sudden destruction cometh upon them, as travail upon a woman with child; and they shall not escape."

In this passage Peter refers us to the End of the 1000 year reign of our Lord Jesus Christ.

2 Peter 3:10, "But the day of the Lord will come as a thief in the night; in the which the heavens shall pass away with a great noise, and the elements shall melt with fervent heat, the earth also and the works that are therein shall be burned up."

Let's look at one more verse, to remove the confusion of those teachings you may have heard, confusing all these events:

Revelation 21:1, "And I saw a new heaven and a new earth: for the first heaven and the first earth were passed away; and there was no more sea."

The Bible is telling us that the Rapture and the ensuing events leading up to the Second Coming of Christ, and His reign, will all happen suddenly. Things will move quickly. As the

Lord told us in Matthew 24, it will be the worst time the earth has ever seen, or will ever see.

The Biblical signs we will mention in this book all point to the Second Coming, when the Lord will step down on the earth (terra firma). He will descend upon the mount of Olives and it will split in half as described in **Zachariah 14:4, "And his feet shall stand in that day upon the mount of Olives, which is before Jerusalem on the east, and the mount of Olives shall cleave in the midst thereof toward the east and toward the west, and there shall be a very great valley; and half of the mountain shall remove toward the north, and half of it toward the south."** Then He will walk up to the Golden (Eastern) Gate which will be opened for Him. From there (Jerusalem) He will rule and reign for 1000 years. We, the Church, will return with Him according to **Jude 1:14, "And Enoch also, the seventh from Adam, prophesied of these, saying, Behold, the Lord cometh with ten thousands of his saints."** We will rule and reign with Christ for 1000 years. **Revelation 20:6, "Blessed and holy is he that hath part in the first resurrection: on such the second death hath no power, but they shall be priests of God and of Christ, and shall reign with him a thousand years."**

There are many ways to know, we are living in the time just before the "Day of the Lord" begins. Let's look at some ways you may have never heard of before.

The Bible tells us that I just as the Second Coming of the Lord has a "fullness" which we will see before He returns, so also there was a "fullness of times" before His first Coming. **Galatians 4:4-5, "But when the fullness of the time was come, God sent forth his Son, made of a woman, made**

under the law, To redeem them that were under the law, that we might receive the adoption of sons."

Scripture is filled with events that are types or shadows of a future event. For an example, Abraham was commanded of God to offer his son Isaac as a sacrifice. This was a test and God would stop him; but as he and his son, Isaac, where walking up to Mount Moriah, Isaac, not knowing what would happen, asked his father, "where is the sacrifice?" **Genesis 22:8, "And Abraham said, My son, God will provide himself a lamb for a burnt offering: so they went both of them together."** Look at even the wording of this text, "God will provide Himself a lamb." He did. Jesus, God's only Son would be "the Lamb of God Who takes away the sin of the world." (John 1:29) Referring back to this Genesis text, Jesus said in John 8:55, **"Your father Abraham rejoiced to see my day: and he saw it, and was glad"**

In Hebrews 11:17-19, it tells us Abraham received Isaac back from the dead (he was as good as dead), **"By faith Abraham, when he was tried, offered up Isaac: and he that had received the promises offered up his only begotten son, Of whom it was said, That in Isaac shall thy seed be called: Accounting that God was able to raise him up, even from the dead; from whence also he received him in a figure."** So, this would explain why the following, seemingly meaningless detail, was written in the same text of the offering of Isaac: **Genesis 22:4, "Then on the third day Abraham lifted up his eyes, and saw the place afar off."** See, for three days, Abraham thought in his mind that his son was as good as dead. But on that 3rd day, he received him back alive! This is one of thousands of examples of God's way of stamping His signature on His work, so we may boldly say, "My God knows all things, from the past to the future eternal, and yet He knows me, just a person living in my little world here, on earth."

If we want to gather understanding of how the signs might come together for the return of our Lord to rule His earth, let's look at the types and shadows of the "fullness of time" that occurred for His First Advent. **Galatians 4:4-5, "But when the fullness of the time was come, God sent forth his Son, made of a woman, made under the law, To redeem them that were under the law, that we might receive the adoption of sons."**

There were many things that came together to prepare the world to receive the Gospel. All were accomplished according to God's purposes, so that Christianity might spread throughout the world, which it did. Had Jesus Christ been born at a different time, things might not have turned out the way they did. The Lord knows the end from the beginning and Christ was born at the exact time in history that was perfectly ordered for the spread of the Gospel. For example:

The Romans built a vast network of roads, so that the Gospel could be carried quickly and safely throughout the Empire.

There was one common language which all educated people throughout the Roman Empire learned to speak, read and write: the Greek Language. This was a "first" since the Tower of Babel, and it helped the Gospel to spread rapidly.

There was relative peace throughout the world at the time Christ was born. A rare thing in human history, which kept the borders opened for travel of the Evangelists, and for communication between the Bishops in each city.

Many brilliant thinkers were born in the time leading up to the birth of Christ, who still influence the world today (but their influence is nothing like Jesus' influence). These Philosophers include men like Plato, Aristotle, Socrates, Epicurus, and Cicero, just to name a few. These men got the Hellenist world asking the right questions: Why am I here? What is the meaning of life? What about an afterlife? The minds of the Gentile world were prepared by God to be open to the Gospel.

Just as all the puzzle pieces were in place for Jesus Christ to be born into this world at just the right moment in history to fulfill God's plan of Salvation and to spread the Gospel, we can also understand that at the End of the Age, everything must fall into place correctly for the Anti-Christ to enter the world scene. The stage must be set for the rise of the Antichrist and his New World Order which will occur, just prior to the Lord's second coming. And that is happening right now.

This book will try and show all the streams that are feeding into the river of the "fullness of times," the tributaries which are merging together at a point, in a confluence which will become a great river that will flood the kingdoms of the world with a 7 year season of one world government know as the Great Tribulation, or the Kingdom of the Antichrist. **Daniel 9:26-27, "And after threescore and two weeks shall Messiah be cut off, but not for himself: and the people of the prince that shall come shall destroy the city and the sanctuary; and the end thereof shall be with a flood, and unto the end of the war desolations are determined. And he shall confirm the covenant with many for one week: and in the midst of the week he shall cause the sacrifice and the oblation to cease, and for the overspreading of abominations he shall make it desolate, even until the consummation, and that determined shall be poured upon the desolate."**

Let us look together at the headwaters of each stream, and follow them to see where they connect with the each other to form this dark river, that the Anti-Christ will ride to power, creating a realm of evil which Jesus Christ described as more terrible than any other time in human history. So that we all will wake up and realize that the text that Israel will lament at the dawn of the Antichrist kingdom will not be spoken from the mouths of our families and friends:

Jeremiah 8:20. "The harvest is past, the summer is ended, and we are not saved."

Jeremiah 8:11-22 "For they have healed the hurt of the daughter of my people slightly, saying, Peace, peace; when there is no peace.[12] Were they ashamed when they had committed abomination? nay, they were not at all ashamed, neither could they blush: therefore shall they fall among them that fall: in the time of their visitation they shall be cast down, saith the Lord.[13] I will surely consume them, saith the Lord: there shall be no grapes on the vine, nor figs on the fig tree, and the leaf shall fade; and the things that I have given them shall pass away from them.[14] Why do we sit still? assemble yourselves, and let us enter into the defenced cities, and let us be silent there: for the Lord our God hath put us to silence, and given us water of gall to drink, because we have sinned against the Lord.[15] We looked for peace, but no good came; and for a time of health, and behold trouble![16] The snorting of his horses was heard from Dan: the whole land trembled at the sound of the neighing of his strong ones; for they are come, and

have devoured the land, and all that is in it; the city, and those that dwell therein.[17] For, behold, I will send serpents, cockatrices, among you, which will not be charmed, and they shall bite you, saith the LORD.[18] When I would comfort myself against sorrow, my heart is faint in me.[19] Behold the voice of the cry of the daughter of my people because of them that dwell in a far country: Is not the LORD in Zion? is not her king in her? Why have they provoked me to anger with their graven images, and with strange vanities?[20] The harvest is past, the summer is ended, and we are not saved.[21] For the hurt of the daughter of my people am I hurt; I am black; astonishment hath taken hold on me.[22] Is there no balm in Gilead; is there no physician there? why then is not the health of the daughter of my people recovered?"

This is a text that will be fulfilled after the start of the tribulation. The one whose horse is heard in Dan is the Antichrist. Most scripture scholars believe that this refers to the tribe of Dan and that it means that the Anti-Christ will have some ancestry from that tribe. This is also alluded to by Jacob on his deathbed prophecy:

"Dan shall be a serpent by the way, an adder in the path, that biteth the horse heels, so that his rider shall fall backward." Genesis 49:17

After reading this book, may it be that the Lord God Almighty would WAKE you, and SHAKE you, and RAISE you up as Lazarus was raised when the Lord called his name! May we, as a Church, be ready to cut the grave clothes off all who awaken in these last days and answer the call of the Lord to COME FORTH!

The biggest problem we face is many will say, "Surely, you're not saying I am asleep?" Yes, *I am* saying that the Western Church is sleeping, cold and dead; even as the devil is deceiving our neighbors, loved ones, and the lukewarm church with trickery, seduction and lies.

May the Lord grant you faith and wisdom as you read this, so that you may be empowered to raise the last alarm for the lost before it is too late! May the fire of the Holy Spirit be ignited in your heart and give you boldness to move out of the safety of your comfort zone and go to the enemy's camp to take that which belongs to our Lord. Namely, the souls of mankind that are blinded to the Gospel of Jesus Christ!

Titus 2:26, "And that they may recover themselves out of the snare of the devil, who are taken captive by him at his will."

May the Lord use this book for His glory!
God Bless you as you read this book,

Patrick Winfrey

Chapter 1

SATAN'S MASTER PLAN

Isaiah 14: 12-14, "How art thou fallen from heaven, O Lucifer, son of the morning! How art thou cut down to the ground, which didst weaken the nations! For thou hast stars of God: I will sit also upon the mount of the congregation, in the sides of the north: I will ascend above the heights of the clouds; I will be like the most High."

S atan, like humanity, was created with free will. Satan, like humanity, chose to rebel against God.

Satan wanted to be like God. Not just "like God", Satan wanted to BE God, to be worshipped. In his rebellion, Satan persuaded one third of the Heavenly Host to rebel with him. These are the fallen angels.

Revelation 12:3-4 "And another sign appeared in heaven: behold, a great, fiery red dragon having seven heads and ten horns, and seven diadems on his heads. His tail drew

a third of the stars (stars are symbolic of angels) of heaven and threw them to the earth..."

This chapter will give a quick review of the history of Satan's work in the Bible; but first we must step out of the natural, or carnal thinking, and into the supernatural, or spiritual thinking.

In Matthew's Gospel, the demons possessing the men in the country of the Gergesenes cried out to Jesus saying **"What have we to do with thee, Jesus, thou Son of God? Art thou come hither to torment us before the time?" (Matthew 8:29)**

The demons knew FOUR things: (1) That there was an appointed time, (2) that they would be tormented at that exact time, (3) that the time was *not* then, and (4) that Jesus was *the* Son of God!

So, too, Satan knows that the Messiah is about to return and he and his band of rebellious fallen angels have been working to interrupt God's Divine plan since the beginning. He uses people as pawns on his chess board in his game to beat God. And just as in a game of chess, a player tries to capture as many pieces from his opponent as possible; Satan is strategizing to "take out" the people of God.

God's FIRST covenant; before Noah, Abraham or Moses, was the family: Adam and Eve. The family is the foundation of human society. If Satan can take out the family, he can do maximum damage to the Kingdom of God. And he can cause maximum benefit to Kingdom of Darkness. Just as our Almighty God and Loving Creator has an ultimate plan for our souls, **the enemy** of our souls, that old serpent, the dragon of old (Revelation 12:9), has a Master plan also. So friends, before we look at the current course and coming kingdom of the devil and his seed, the Anti-Christ, let's look at the history of how old slew foot tried to thwart The Master's plans through history.

The basic unit of society that God ordained in the Garden was the family. Not a President of the United States of America and his wife, but Adam and Eve, are the real "First Family." The first covenant was made with them, by our God, the Creator. Many Christians believe that The Church, as the Bride of Christ, is a reflection of that first husband and wife, Adam and Eve. The Lord uses this language in the Bible about the Church as a expression of the marriage between that first couple, Adam and Eve.

(Ephesians 5:23, "For the husband is the head of the wife, even as Christ is the head of the church: and he is the saviour of the body.")

The union of husband and wife which God ordain and created in the garden, and all marriages since, are a lesser light, a reflection on earth, of His kingdom in Heaven. Marriage is patterned after the Lord and His bride the Church! **Thy will be done on earth, as it is in heaven.** Just as the Lord told Moses concerning the construction of the Tabernacle in the wilderness, MAKE IT AFTER THE PATTERN YOU SAW IN HEAVEN. **(Exodus 25:40, "And look that thou make them after their pattern, which was shewed thee in the mount.")**

Let's go deeper. Jesus said He was doing on earth what He saw His Father doing in Heaven. **John 5:19-20, "Then answered Jesus and said unto them, Verily, verily, I say unto you, The Son can do nothing of himself, but what he seeth the Father do: for what things soever he doeth, these also doeth the Son likewise. For the Father loveth**

23

the Son, and sheweth him all things that himself doeth: and he will shew him greater works than these, that ye may marvel." Jesus goes on to explain in this text that just as He was doing on earth what His Father was doing in heaven; those Israelites, who were rejecting Him, were doing what *their father*, the devil, does.

It has been famously said, Satan's greatest work has been convincing people he does not exist. This is a truth we must begin to get into our hearts and spirits if we are to overcome our natural, fleshly blindness to the spiritual world around us. The Bible says Satan blinds people to spiritual truth.

2 Corinthians 4:3-4, "But if our gospel be hid, it is hid to them that are lost: In whom the god of this world hath blinded the minds of them which believe not, lest the light of the glorious gospel of Christ, who is the image of God, should shine unto them."

Jesus said in Luke 4:18 that the Spirit of the Lord was upon Him to open the eyes of the blind. **"The Spirit of the Lord is upon me, because he hath anointed me to preach the gospel to the poor; he hath sent me to heal the bro-kenhearted, to preach deliverance to the captives, and recovering of sight to the blind, to set at liberty them that are bruised"**

He also said: John 9:39-41 **"And Jesus said, For judg-ment I am come into this world, that they which see not might see; and that they which see might be made blind. And *some* of the Pharisees which were with him heard these words, and said unto him, Are we blind also?"** Jesus

said unto them, If ye were blind, ye should have no sin:
but now ye say, We see; therefore your sin remaineth."

Let's look at more biblical texts to assure ourselves, that
the spirit world is more real than this one, and the two worlds
move as one, whether good or bad, Divine or demonic.

2 Kings 6:15-18 :
**"And when the servant of the man of God was risen early,
and gone forth, behold, an host compassed the city both
with horses and chariots. And his servant said unto him,
'Alas, my master! how shall we do?' And he answered, 'Fear
not: for they that *be* with us *are* more than they that *be*
with them.' And Elisha prayed, and said, 'LORD, I pray thee,
open his eyes, that he may see.' And the LORD opened
the eyes of the young man; and he saw: and, behold, the
mountain *was* full of horses and chariots of fire round
about Elisha. And when they came down to him, Elisha
prayed unto the LORD, and said, 'Smite this people, I pray
thee, with blindness.' And he smote them with blindness
according to the word of Elisha."**

The Last two texts, Elisha and the servant and Jesus and
the blind man, show that blindness and sight, whether spiritual
or physical, are in God's Hand. I pray that the Lord will use this
book to help you to have your spiritual eyes open more and
more, so that you can be used by the Lord to help others get
free from that wicked enemy of our souls.

In the text of Elisha, we see, the spirit world is working
with the nature world. Elisha prayed for his servant to see in

both worlds, and that the enemies of God would be blinded in both worlds!

Now that we have some biblical background to get us thinking spiritually, rather than like the servant of Elisha, let's cross into the deep end of the river of the Lord.

Ezekiel 47:1-5:
"Afterward he brought me again unto the door of the house; and, behold, waters issued out from under the threshold of the house eastward: for the forefront of the house stood toward the east, and the waters came down from under from the right side of the house, at the south side of the altar. Then brought he me out of the way of the gate northward, and led me about the way without unto the utter gate by the way that looketh eastward; and, behold, there ran out waters on the right side. And when the man that had the line in his hand went forth eastward, he measured a thousand cubits, and he brought me through the waters; the waters were to the ankles. Again he measured a thousand, and brought me through the waters; the waters were to the knees. Again he measured a thousand, and brought me through; the waters were to the loins. Afterward he measured a thousand; and it was a river that I could not pass over: for the waters were risen, waters to swim in, a river that could not be passed over.

The "house" in this text is the Temple. The Temple is the "start point of religion", The Word of God. The farther out we go into the Holy Spirit, the deeper the river of God becomes. But, all wisdom and anointing flows from the base, the Temple, the

Word of God. To go into deep water requires getting in "over your head", so that only His Grace is carrying us, imparting wisdom and understanding into deeper spiritual truths. It is the work of the Holy Spirit to do this. John 7:38, tell us, **"He that believeth on me, as the scripture hath said, out of his belly shall flow rivers of living water."** And John 16:13 says, **"Howbeit when he, the Spirit of truth, is come, he will guide you into all truth: for he shall not speak of himself; but whatsoever he shall hear, that shall he speak: and he will shew you things to come."** If we desire wisdom and understanding, we need only to ask the Holy Spirit living within us and He will enlighten our hearts and open our spiritual eyes to understand the deeper things of God. **James 1:5, "If any of you lack wisdom, let him ask of God, that giveth to all men liberally, and upbraideth not; and it shall be given him."**

Luke 11:14-26 :

"**And he was casting out a devil, and it was dumb. And it came to pass, when the devil was gone out, the dumb spake; and the people wondered.**[15] **But some of them said, He casteth out devils through Beelzebub the chief of the devils.**[16] **And others, tempting him, sought of him a sign from heaven.**[17] **But he, knowing their thoughts, said unto them, Every kingdom divided against itself is brought to desolation; and a house divided against a house falleth.**[18] **If Satan also be divided against himself, how shall his kingdom stand? because ye say that I cast out devils through Beelzebub.**[19] **And if I by Beelzebub cast out devils, by whom do your sons cast them out? therefore shall they be your judges.**[20] **But if I with the finger of God cast out**

devils, no doubt the <u>kingdom of God is come</u> upon you.[21] **When a strong man armed keepeth his palace, his goods are in peace:**[22] **But when a stronger than he shall come upon him, and overcome him, he taketh from him all his armour wherein he trusted, and divideth his spoils.**[23] **He that is not with me is against me: and he that gathereth not with me scattereth.**[24] **When the unclean spirit is gone out of a man, he walketh through dry places, seeking rest; and finding none, he saith, I will return unto my house whence I came out.**[25] **And when he cometh, he findeth it swept and garnished.**[26] **Then goeth he, and taketh to him seven other spirits more wicked than himself; and they enter in, and dwell there: and the last state of that man is worse than the first."**

Every time someone gets saved, the Kingdom of God has come near! When someone is healed, the Kingdom of God has come near! His will has been done on earth, as it is in heaven! There are no lost there, or sick!

Luke 15:10, "Likewise, I say unto you, there is joy in the presence of the angels of God over one sinner that repenteth."

Let's look at one more example of parallels between the spiritual world and the natural world. **Genesis 2:7, "And the Lord God formed man of the dust of the ground, and breathed into his nostrils the breath of life; and man became a living soul."** Adam, the name, actually means "red clay/dirt." **John 7:38**, tells us, **"He that believeth on me, as the scripture**

28

hath said, out of his belly shall flow rivers of living water."
Water represents the Holy Spirit. Bear in mind for this example
that "dirt" represents the natural world, humanity, and "water"
represents the spiritual world, the work of the Holy Spirit.

John 9:1-7:
**"And as Jesus passed by, he saw a man which was blind
from his birth.[2] And his disciples asked him, saying, Master,
who did sin, this man, or his parents, that he was born
blind?[3] Jesus answered, Neither hath this man sinned, nor
his parents: but that the works of God should be made
manifest in him.[4] I must work the works of him that sent
me, while it is day: the night cometh, when no man can
work.[5] As long as I am in the world, I am the light of the
world.[6] When he had thus spoken, he spat on the ground,
and made clay of the spittle, and he anointed the eyes of
the blind man with the clay,[7] And said unto him, Go, wash
in the pool of Siloam, (which is by interpretation, Sent.)
He went his way therefore, and washed, and came seeing."**

Here our Lord Jesus took water, representing the Holy Spirit,
from His mouth and mixed it with clay or dirt from the ground,
representing the natural world or humanity. He put this mixture
on the eyes of the blind man, and when the man washed his
eyes in the pool, he was healed of his blindness.

John 9:32-34 :
**"Since the world began was it not heard that any man
opened the eyes of one that was born blind.[33] If this man
were not of God, he could do nothing.[34] They answered**

and said unto him, Thou wast altogether born in sins, and dost thou teach us? And they cast him out."

After being questioned by the religious officials, the once-blind man was kicked out of the synagogue. When Jesus found out about it, He asked the man if he believed in the Son of Man. The man asked Jesus "who is He that I might believe?" And Jesus said, "I am He." When the man who had been healed of his physical blindness realized Jesus was the Messiah, he fell down and worshiped at His feet. Jesus had healed his physical blindness.

Now let's look at the spiritual blindness. Jesus continues speaking, **John 9:39-41, "And Jesus said, For judgment I am come into this world, that they which see not might see; and that they which see might be made blind.⁴⁰ And some of the Pharisees which were with him heard these words, and said unto him, Are we blind also? ⁴¹ Jesus said unto them, If ye were blind, ye should have no sin: but now ye say, We see; therefore your sin remaineth."**

The Pharisees recognized that Jesus was saying they were spiritually blind. They were offended at what He said but they still did not "get it." Why? Because 2 Corinthians 4:4 tells us, **"In whom the god of this world hath blinded the minds of them which believe not, lest the light of the glorious gospel of Christ, who is the image of God, should shine unto them."** The Pharisees of Jesus' day, like many in our day, had been blinded by "the god of this world" so that they could not see the Light of the World.

John 10:1-2, "Verily, verily, I say unto you, He that entereth not by the door into the sheepfold, but climbeth

up some other way, the same is a thief and a robber.[2] But he
that entereth in by the door is the shepherd of the sheep."
Jesus is still speaking about the miracle healing of the man
who had been blind from birth as John 10 begins. **John 10:7,
"Then said Jesus unto them again, Verily, verily, I say unto
you, I am the door of the sheep."**

God has an ordered plan of Salvation. In Adam all died, but
in Christ shall we be made alive. First the natural: Adam's sin.
Then the spiritual: Christ's redemption.

1 Corinthians 15:45-55:

**"And so it is written, The first man Adam was made a living
soul; the last Adam was made a quickening spirit.[46] Howbeit
that was not first which is spiritual, but that which is natural;
and afterward that which is spiritual.[47] The first man is of the
earth, earthy; the second man is the Lord from heaven.[48]
As is the earthy, such are they also that are earthy: and as
is the heavenly, such are they also that are heavenly.[49] And
as we have borne the image of the earthy, we shall also
bear the image of the heavenly.[50] Now this I say, brethren,
that flesh and blood cannot inherit the kingdom of God;
neither doth corruption inherit incorruption.[51] Behold, I
shew you a mystery; We shall not all sleep, but we shall
all be changed,[52] In a moment, in the twinkling of an eye, at
the last trump: for the trumpet shall sound, and the dead
shall be raised incorruptible, and we shall be changed.[53] For
this corruptible must put on incorruption, and this mortal
must put on immortality.[54] So when this corruptible shall
have put on incorruption, and this mortal shall have put
on immortality, then shall be brought to pass the saying**

that is written, Death is swallowed up in victory.[55]**O death, where is thy sting? O grave, where is thy victory?"**

Jesus took the clay, representing man, and put it over the eyes of the blind man. This represents God coming in the flesh. Then Jesus began explaining that He came through the door of the sheepfold, through the flesh. Jesus followed the rules. He took on flesh and blood to pay the price of our redemption. He did not descend from Heaven in all of His Divine Glory, but He humbled Himself, and became a servant, so that He might fulfill the plan of Salvation for humanity.

Satan will not follow the rules. He never has. Fallen angels, aliens, they will trick people, they will descend from heaven like angels (or like aliens), they will attempt to mix DNA. They will not follow God's rules of order. Jesus came in the FLESH, God manifested in the flesh. His DNA was human; Christ did not descend from heaven like an angel. As Jesus said in **John 10:12, "But he that entereth in by the door is the shepherd of the sheep."** We can understand that the "door" the Lord is referring to is the flesh, the authorized door God made to enter this world. This is why demons try to possess people. They are trying to climb into this physical, three-dimensional world, by another way.

This is also why we are convinced, although it is not the primary topic of this book, that the beings which many believe to be extra-terrestrial aliens have abducted hundreds of thousands of people around the world. This is why these abductees claim to have been subjected to medical experimentation and testing that so often is reported as having a sexual or reproductive focus. Perhaps a type of human-alien hybridization is taking place so that when the Nephalim return, it will not be as it was in **Genesis 6:4, "when the sons of God came in unto the daughters of men, and they bare children to them, the same became mighty men which were of old, men of renown,"** but rather the spirits of the original Nephalim returning in a host body. Creatures of altered human DNA!

Those who study "alien abduction" cases have found an abundance of evidence to support the stories of the victims. It seems, this maybe the way the Antichrist will find himself literally Apollyon-possessed after his seemingly fatal head wound in the middle of the Tribulation. Could this be the spiritual battle the world will see during the tribulation? However it unfolds, this battle will be the worst event that mankind has ever, or will ever see. **"For then shall be great tribulation, such as was not since the beginning of the world to this time, no, nor ever shall be." Matthew 24:21.** Please make sure you are ready now, so that you can "escape all these things that shall come to pass, and to stand before the Son of man" at the Rapture of the Church. Luke 21:36.

Matthew 11:12: "And from the days of John the Baptist until now the kingdom of heaven suffereth violence, and the violent take it by force."

Just as there was a spiritual battle that reached an apex in the time of the First Coming of the Lord; and it is happening again as the Second Coming of the Lord, and His final victory draws near. The violence in the spiritual world is increasing, while the natural world is being sung to sleep by the devil. The enemy is trying to keep us busy with the things of this world, but the Lord is calling us by His Spirit, "COME UP HERE, and I will show you what is really happening. He is saying to us, like he did the blind man; LET ME OPEN YOUR EYES." Once we understand what is going on around us, we can begin to ignore the flesh and blood that fights us and focus on the spiritual force behind it. Within ourselves we can never defeat the spiritual enemies, but the battle is the Lord's. If God be for us, who can be against us? We are called to fight the good fight of FAITH!

Satan and the hosts of Hell have always wanted to persuade humanity to worship Lucifer, just as he persuaded one-third of the angels. This began in the Garden of Eden, when taking the form of a serpent, he beguiled Eve with the words "ye shall not surely die" (Genesis 3:4); enticing her to eat of the fruit of the tree of Knowledge of Good and Evil with the promise that when she did, she would become like God. "You can become a god" is Satan's master wisdom, his master plan to slap God in the face by corrupting humanity which was made in His (God's) image.

Yet, at the fall of man, God promised redemption.

Genesis 3:15:
"And I will put enmity between thee and the woman, and between thy seed and her seed; it shall bruise thy head, and thou shalt bruise his heel."

As soon as Satan understood the prophecy of Genesis 3:15, he began trying to stop it. Satan and his fallen angels began working to interrupt God's plan of redemption for humanity. Satan tried his best to stop the arrival of the Messiah.

Genesis 6:4-9:

"There were giants in the earth in those days; and also after that, when the sons of God came in unto the daughters of men, and they bare children to them, the same became mighty men which were of old, men of renown.[5] And God saw that the wickedness of man was great in the earth, and that every imagination of the thoughts of his heart was only evil continually.[6] And it repented the Lord that he had made man on the earth, and it grieved him at his heart.[7] And the Lord said, I will destroy man whom I have created from the face of the earth; both man, and beast, and the creeping thing, and the fowls of the air; for it repenteth me that I have made them.[8] But Noah found grace in the eyes of the Lord.[9] These are the generations of Noah: Noah was a just man and perfect in his generations, and Noah walked with God."

Before we can push deeper into truth, we must first look at some standard interpretations and see if they make sense in light of biblical truth:

There is a theory that comes from the 4th century school of thought developed by St. Augustine, a Roman Catholic theologian, who taught that if a literal interpretation of the Bible was not readily apparent, then an allegorical interpretation of Biblical text was necessary. The result was hundreds of years of allegorical teaching of scripture that should be taken literally. Most notably, St. Augustine's theory of scripture interpretation gave rise to what is known as "replacement theology" in which "Israel" is replaced by the "Church" and "Jerusalem" is replaced by "Heaven." Here is the irony: (and would be humorous if it would not leave billions who will be left behind at the Rapture woefully ignorant of the strong delusion ascending out of the bottomless pit to snare the masses into taking the Mark of the Beast, thus condemning themselves to an eternity in the Lake of Fire) most Evangelical seminaries, having rejected the long-held allegorical teaching of "replacement theology" for a literal interpretation of almost all the Bible, still hold to Augustinian interpretation of this text from Genesis.

Another idea taught by these Evangelical scholars is known as the "Sons of Seth Theory." It is said that the "sons of God" in Genesis 6:4 are the descendants of Seth, and the "daughters of men", are the descendants of Cain. This theory not only violates their own standard of biblical interpretation, but makes no logical sense. If Seth's sons were the "sons of God," why did they all perish in the flood except Noah? Why would Genesis 6:4 clearly state **"There were giants in the earth in those days; and also <u>after </u>that, when the sons of God came in unto the daughters of men, and they bare children to them, the same became mighty men which were of old, men of renown"**? In the Genesis 4 narrative, "in those days" refers to the days of Noah, "and after that" is speaking times AFTER Noah. The "sons of Seth" theory does nothing to address the plain text which clearly states "there were *giants* in the earth." If descendants of Seth were good people who married descendants of Cain who were bad people, how can their descendants be "giants," or men of renowned?

By analyzing this scripture in light of Satan's plan to stop the seed of the woman from bringing forth the Messiah, and by assuming the plain sense of the scripture should make sense, we begin to see a truth that perhaps the Lord has allowed to remain concealed until these Last Days. Just as the Holy Spirit has been slowly restoring His Church back to sound doctrine since the time of the Reformation; He will lead and guide those who sincerely seek the Truth.

The confusion seems to be, that in the New Testament, the "Sons of God", refers to Christians. In the Old Testament, all references to the "Sons of God" are about angels. **Job 1:6, "Now there was a day when the sons of God came to present themselves before the L**ORD**, and Satan came also among them."**

Jude 1:6 states, **"And the angels which kept not their first estate, but left their own habitation, he hath reserved in everlasting chains under darkness unto the judgment of the great day."** These are fallen angels obviously, because God has reserved "everlasting chains under darkness" for them. Jude tells us, and he is quoting the book of Enoch when he does so, that these angels did not remain in the second heaven, but went where they did not belong. These fallen angels who "kept not their first estate" are the "sons of God" who "came into the daughters of men and they bare children to them", who were the "mighty men of old", the giants spoken of in Genesis account of the flood and in many other Old Testament references. The scriptures below are but a small sample:

- **Numbers 13:33:** "The sons of Anak, which come of the **giants,"**
- **Deuteronomy 2:20-21:** "That also was accounted a land of **giants: giants** dwelt therein in old time; and the Ammonites call them Zamzummims; A people great, and many, and tall, as the Anakims; but the L**ORD** destroyed

them before them; and they succeeded them, and dwelt in their stead,"

- **Deuteronomy 3:11:** "For only Og king of Bashan remained of the remnant of **giants**; behold his bedstead was a bedstead of iron; is it not in Rabbath of the children of Ammon? nine cubits was the length thereof, and four cubits the breadth of it, after the cubit of a man."
- **Joshua 15:8:** "valley of the **giants**"
- **Joshua 17:15:** "land of the Perizzites and of the **giants**"

These were not metaphorical giants, these were actual, physically large and strong people, such as Og, King of Bashan whose bed was approximately 14 feet long, and 6 feet wide. When Moses sent the 12 spies into the land of Canaan, 10 of them came back with a fearful report because there were *giants* in the land. **"And there we saw the giants, the sons of Anak, which come of the giants: and we were in our own sight as grasshoppers, and so we were in their sight" Numbers 13:33.** The account of the terrified spies was not just hyperbole. They saw *actual giants* in the land of Canaan and they were so afraid that they did not trust God to give them the Promised Land.

Satan and his fallen angels ("sons of God") seduced the women of earth ("daughters of men") and the offspring of that unholy matrimony was a race of giants. Knowing that the Savior would be from the "seed of the woman", Satan lost no time in trying to corrupt that seed and stop the plan of Salvation by contaminating the bloodline of the Messiah. But we see that Noah's bloodline was not corrupted, he was from a family that had not mingled with the fallen angels: he was "perfect in his *generations.*" The word "generations" is plural, not singular, so it is referring to the ancestry of Noah. Not only was Noah walking with God in his generation (singular) as an example to his wicked and perverse peers; but he came from a family (generations, plural) that had not intermarried with the race of giants.

Of course we all know the story of Noah and the flood, how it rained for 40 days and water covered the earth for a year. When the flood waters abated, God set His rainbow in the clouds as a token of His promise to never destroy earth by flood again. **Genesis 9:1, "And God blessed Noah and his sons, and said unto them, Be fruitful, and multiply, and replenish the earth."**

Noah and his family were to leave the ark and spread out all over the world to "replenish the earth." They finally did obey God's command for scripture tells us in Genesis 9:19, **"These are the three sons of Noah: and of them was the whole earth overspread."** But they did not obey right away. They stayed very close to the mountain on which the ark landed. Genesis 11:1-4, **"And it came to pass, as they journeyed from the east, that they found a plain in the land of Shinar; and they dwelt there. And they said one to another, Go to, let us make brick, and burn them thoroughly. And they had brick for stone, and slime had they for morter. And they said, Go to, let us build us a city and a tower, whose top may reach unto heaven; and let us make us a name, lest we be scattered abroad upon the face of the whole earth."**

Satan enticed the people of Babel to build a tower to reach Heaven. Satan is still persuading people today that they can get to Heaven by themselves, in their own way, that they can by-pass the plan of Salvation through Jesus Christ.

Satan seems to have the ability to see into the future, at least in a limited way. When Moses was about to be born, Satan tried to stop it by having Pharaoh enact harsh laws, including requiring midwives to dispose of male Hebrew babies in the Nile River. Perhaps Satan thought that Moses was to be the Messiah, or perhaps he knew that Moses was to deliver God's people from Egyptian slavery and that these people (the Hebrews) were in the bloodline of the Messiah. Certainly Satan did all that was within his power to prevent the birth of Moses.

Yet God's Will always prevails. Not only was Moses kept safe, hidden in a basket among the bulrushes of the Nile; but Pharaoh's daughter found him and paid his own mother to be his wet-nurse. God arranged for Moses to be raised in Pharaoh's palace and receive the best possible Egyptian education as well.

The Lord gave the prophet Zechariah insight into how Satan operates when He related the vision described in Zechariah 3:1-4, **"And he shewed me Joshua the high priest standing before the angel of the Lord, and Satan standing at his right hand to resist him. And the Lord said unto Satan, The Lord rebuke thee, O Satan; even the Lord that hath chosen Jerusalem rebuke thee: is not this a brand plucked out of the fire? Now Joshua was clothed with filthy garments, and stood before the angel. And he answered and spake unto those that stood before him, saying, Take away the filthy garments from him. And unto him he said, Behold, I have caused thine iniquity to pass from thee, and I will clothe thee with change of raiment."**

Here we are told that Satan accused Joshua the high priest before the Lord because Joshua was clothed with filthy garments. But the Lord rebuked Satan. God took away the high priest's filthy garments **("But we are all as an unclean thing, and all our righteousnesses are as filthy rags; and we all do fade as a leaf; and our iniquities, like the wind, have taken us away." Isaiah 64:6)** and gave him a new set of clothes. God let Zechariah see a glimpse into the spiritual world as to how the plan of salvation was going to be carried out in the lives of the redeemed. (God exchanges our filthy rags for robes of righteousness through Christ Jesus.) But he also was given an insight into how the darker side of the spirit world works, how the devil accuses the redeemed before God.

Satan appears again in scripture in **Matthew 4:1-11**:

"Then was Jesus led up of the Spirit into the wilderness to be tempted of the devil.[2] **And when he had fasted forty days and forty nights, he was afterward an hungred.**[3] **And when the tempter came to him, he said, If thou be the Son of God, command that these stones be made bread.**[4] **But he answered and said, It is written, Man shall not live by bread alone, but by every word that proceedeth out of the mouth of God.**[5] **Then the devil taketh him up into the holy city, and setteth him on a pinnacle of the temple,**[6] **And saith unto him, If thou be the Son of God, cast thyself down: for it is written, He shall give his angels charge concerning thee: and in their hands they shall bear thee up, lest at any time thou dash thy foot against a stone.**[7] **Jesus said unto him, It is written again, Thou shalt not tempt the Lord thy God.**[8] **Again, the devil taketh him up into an exceeding high mountain, and sheweth him all the kingdoms of the world, and the glory of them;**[9] **And saith unto him, All these things will I give thee, if thou wilt fall down and worship**

me.[10] **Then saith Jesus unto him, Get thee hence, Satan: for it is written, Thou shalt worship the Lord thy God, and him only shalt thou serve.[11] Then the devil leaveth him, and, behold, angels came and ministered unto him."**

Notice the temptation tactics Satan used against Jesus: from the most basic human need of food, to fame (what notoriety Jesus would have when everyone witnessed his death defying leap from the pinnacle of the temple!) and power. This final offering, power/authority, would have the highest price tag: "fall down and worship me." Interestingly, Jesus did not rebuke Satan by telling him he was lying about his ability to bestow the "kingdoms of the world" in exchange for worship; and this is a good indication that Satan *does indeed* have authority over these kingdoms. Ephesians 2:2 calls Satan "the **prince of the power** of the air." In John 14:30, our Lord Himself says" the **prince of this world** cometh, and hath nothing in me." Satan *is* the prince of this world and *does* exercise authority over the kingdoms of this world.

We see Satan again at the Last Supper, **"When Jesus had thus said, he was troubled in spirit, and testified, and said, Verily, verily, I say unto you, that one of you shall betray me."** (John 13:21) The account continues, **"He then lying on Jesus' breast saith unto him, Lord, who is it?[26] Jesus answered, He it is, to whom I shall give a sop, when I have dipped it. And when he had dipped the sop, he gave it to Judas Iscariot, the son of Simon.[27] And after the sop <u>Satan entered into him</u>. Then said Jesus unto him, That thou doest, do quickly." John 13:25-27**

It is clear from this passage that the devil entered into Judas Iscariot; Satan possessed him, so that he would betray Jesus into the hands of the Jewish leaders. This is another example of the powers of darkness having some, but not all, knowledge of God's plans. 1 Corinthians 2:7-8 tells us, **"But we speak the wisdom of God in a mystery, even the hidden wisdom, which God ordained before the world unto our glory:**[8] **Which none of the princes of this world knew: for had they known it, they would not have crucified the Lord of glory."** Satan thought that he would be able to derail the Plan of Salvation for humanity by having Jesus crucified, when in actuality, the devil was doing exactly what God had ordained.

We will come back to the Church Age toward the end of the book, after we examine what Satan has done to bring the once-Christian nation of the United States to its near destruction today, and then we will try to determine what, if anything, we the Church can do to reverse the damage, to cause our Lord to delay His judgment, and to bring a New Great Awakening in this twilight hour of the Church Age.

Chapter 2

SATAN'S SAGES

James 1:5, "If any of you lack wisdom, let him ask of God, that giveth to all men liberally, and upbraideth not; and it shall be given him."

od has created and inspired all good things. **"Every good gift and every perfect gift is from above, and cometh down from the Father of lights, with whom is no variableness, neither shadow of turning" James 1:17.** Every topic covered in this books leads to the discovery that Satan, The Father of Lies, tries to imitate what God is doing and pervert what God has created. Webster's Dictionary defines a sage a "profoundly wise person; a person famed for wisdom; someone who possesses wisdom, judgment, and experience." But Colossians 2:3 reveals that in CHRIST "are hid all the treasures of wisdom and knowledge." Satan's Sages do possess wisdom, but **"This wisdom descendeth not from above, but is earthly, sensual, devilish. For where envying and strife is, there is confusion and every evil work." James 3:15-16.**

One of the ways we can have a good idea of what may happen as the Kingdom of Antichrist (or New World Order) rises, and what the world's elite are planning to do, is to simply read. They write books that outline their plans. These plans are referred to as "white papers." A White Paper is a definitive position paper on a plan of action issued to test the climate of public opinion concerning a policy issue so that a government can determine its possible impact.(1) One of the most famous examples is *Mein Kampf*, which is German for "My Struggle." This was the White Paper written by Adolf Hitler. Hitler wrote his book in 1923 while he was in prison for political crimes. It was published in 1925, and a second volume in 1926. (2)

In *Mein Kampf* Hitler laid out his plans to bring about a New World Order. He described the problems he thought were hurting the German people and stopping them from ruling the world (as he thought they should because he believed them to be the "Master Race"). Hitler believed that the two biggest problems were Communism and Judaism. He also thought that the parliamentary system should be completely eliminated, saying that it was totally corrupt because the most powerful legislators were always opportunists. His book also described his plan to expand German territory by taking land from Russia, Czechoslovakia and Poland.

Hitler became rich from *Mein Kampf* and was able to finance some of his own political moves with proceeds from its sale. In fact, he made 1.2 million Marks in 1933 alone, an amount of money equal to over $18 million US Dollars today.

Hitler with his book, *Mein Kampf*, is an excellent example for us to develop the idea of how Satan's apostles can be found and their plans and beliefs traced from their very own writings. First, Hitler wrote what he was planning to do. Second, Hitler carried out the plans he had put in writing. The infamous atrocities of Adolph Hitler have shown us that the world should take people like him extremely seriously. After Adolph Hitler's rise to power, Winston Churchill spoke of Hitler's *Mein Kamf* his book, *The Second World War*, saying, "No other book deserved more intensive scrutiny". If people had taken Hitler seriously in 1926, when he published his book, or even in 1933 when he rose to power, he could have been stopped. Germany did not have a military at the time, so it took several more years for Hitler to be able to make war.

This is the first point I am trying to make: Evil men have written their plans for a New World Order. They build upon each others' ideas. Even Hitler, who is a foreshadowing of the Antichrist, was not the first person to have the idea of a "master race", or of ruling the world. In fact, these Ideas go back to Genesis 10-11, back to Nimrod and the Tower of Babel. But let's just limit our study to modern times; otherwise, we could never finish the list of wicked people who have contrived to rule the world by force according to the will of Satan, the Master of Evil.

We can get some idea of what the Antichrist's kingdom will look like, and how he will fool the world, by gleaning from Hitler and his book. Hitler fooled most of his people, and wrought destruction on a scale never before seen in history, a death toll of 60-80 million people, as a result of one man's demon possessed fantasies. So too will the Antichrist rise to power on a platform of peace, but bring about the most devastating annihilation of humanity the world has ever seen.

John 10:10, "The thief cometh not, but for to steal, and to kill, and to destroy: I am come that they might have life, and that they might have it more abundantly."

Most people would be surprised to know that Hitler got many of his ideas from America, especially the concept of a "master race." The majority do not know that eugenics (killing off the weak) was actually promoted in the USA even before Hitler was born. Let's look at the modern root of this evil. You are about to read REAL history never taught in school; because, in these Last Days, our public schools are controlled by Satan and his people.

One of Satan's best sages was Charles Darwin. His theories have done much harm, and have helped lead to the death of 100's of millions. "Survival of the Fittest", a concept directly lifted from Darwin's work, was the prevailing principle which drove Adolph Hitler's atrocities. Hitler believed that some people were "weaker" (inferior races) and that those weaker people should be eliminated so that the "master race", the Arians, would be pure, not mixed with weaker peoples. This idea led the world into war (World War II), and is the core conviction underlying the legalization of abortion. Darwin taught in his book, *The Origin of the Species*, the concept of survival of the fittest, that some are superior to others, that there is a "master race."

Modern day transhumanism is attempting to accomplish the very same goal, that of a "master race." Researchers are developing computer chips that can be implanted into our bodies to alter our DNA. These genetic changes could be used to cure diseases such as Type I (childhood onset) Diabetes or even to genetically modify humans for super sight. For example, experiments are now taking place to try to give cat eye DNA to soldiers, so they can see in the dark.(3) We believe it is entirely possible that the Mark of the Beast will utilize this technology to create super humans, such as those depicted in many of the new movies released in 2013 ("Batman, the Dark Knight Returns," "Iron Man 3," "Man of Steel," and "The Wolverine" as of this writing).

Genesis 3:4-5, "And the serpent said unto the woman, Ye shall not surely die: For God doth know that in the day ye eat thereof, then your eyes shall be opened, and <u>ye shall be as gods</u>, knowing good and evil."

Satan is marketing his same old lies. They are merely repackaged into "new and improved" containers for each successive generation.

It was 1925 when the famous Scopes Monkey Trial made it legal to teach Darwin's Theory of Evolution in the United States. However, since local school boards control curriculums nationwide, few schools actually taught evolution. But in 1958, in the middle of the cold war, many feared that the United States was falling behind the Soviet Union in its education system. The National Defense Education Act was passed and the result was high school textbooks which stressed Darwin's Theory of Evolution as the unifying principle of biology. (4) Darwin's theory has been a boondoggle of hate to justify millions of young People turning away from God and embracing a culture of immorality. Think about it: Why are kids killing each other in school? Why the ever-increasing levels of out of wedlock births, suicides, and drug use? Why do we have mega increases in youths being medicated for mental illness? (Just to name a few.) Because they have been told, they evolved from monkeys. They are animals: No hope. No future. No God. No judgment. No consequences. Only "survival of the fittest." Get yours and step on anyone who stands in your way of happiness. Do you own will. What do we expect young people to do? If there are no moral absolutes, no right or wrong choices; then "might makes right" in the devil's world.

Now let's look at some more White Papers. The devil is the master of deception, and wants you to think he is only a myth. But, that old snake, **"that old serpent, called the Devil, and Satan, which deceives the whole world" (Revelation 12:9)** even had his own "white paper" written in 1904, in Cairo, after a magic ceremony in the King's Chamber of the Great Pyramid.

"Do your own thing" or "do what you want" came straight from Satan's mouth to the ear of the man who was pronounced the most evil man alive in his day. Most now have never heard of him. He is the father of the term "New Age" (eon), which is the devil's main theology. He is also the author of the devil's own "white paper." The initials of his name, ironically, are A.C. Aleister Crowley was his name. He also wrote much about how the world will be taken over. But, unlike Hitler, who wrote how he would do it, or Darwin who wrote about why the world is taken over by the fittest, Aleister Crowley wrote exactly how the devil would bring in the New Age and the kingdom of the Anti-Christ. He was, perhaps, *the most* influential man in the ushering in of the New Age. Let's look at the ideas Satan used Aleister Crowley to introduce to the popular culture through his writings.

Aleister Crowley called himself "The Beast", and the voice he heard was that of a spirit whom he called Horus. Aleister

Crowley wrote down what Horus said in a book entitled "The Book of the Law. [*Liber al vel Legis]*" By reading this book, it is clear to discern that "Horus", who dictated *The Book of the Law* to Crowley, was Satan himself. Aleister Crowley said he wrote what he heard whispered in his ear. His book is filled with all the New Age lies we hear today. New and various want-to-be-guru's of the New Age are just repeating what originated on that fateful trip to Egypt by Crowley. Just as God, in the Bible, records 10 Commandments; Satan, in "The Book of the Law", gave only one: "Do What Thou Wilt, Shall Be the Whole of the Law". Do *your own* will!

Inspired by Satan, Aleister Crowley wrote that the family and Christianity are the biggest enemies of the New Age. And he laid out the plans to destroy both. He called sodomy the "best practice" for the world. He said that women's rights would also help to destroy the family. He advocated drug use. He even wrote a book of poems about being high on cocaine and his homosexual sex acts. He practiced something called "sex magic," believing that the devil's power could be invoked and harnessed much more effectively during rituals to call forth demons which utilized perverted sex as part of the ceremony. Without describing the details of the ceremonies (since this is a Christian book), it is enough to note that animals, and even children, were involved.

"The Book of the Law" was written in 1904. In this book, Crowley laid out *his* master's plan to destroy the family in order to bring in that New Eon, or New Age. It described all the things we saw unfold in the 1960's, the twentieth century's worst-of-all-decade for moral decline. So we see that it was 60 years earlier that the plans were laid for that moral decay. In the 1960's Satan began to implement his campaign to destroy the USA by destroying the Church and the Family. Sex, drugs, Rock-n-Roll, Woman's Liberation, which led to the walking away from responsibilities of family for the devil's lie that material possessions equals happiness. That so-called American dream, of two cars, three TV's, etc, has left the family broken and pursuing false happiness, through fleeting earthly materialism. In the 1960's people began turning from the Lord and from social boundaries, and started running straight into the arms of Satan's Sages.

Remember, that the West was a far different place in 1904, than it is today, a much more moral society, where even the appearance of evil was shunned. My Great Grandma, who was born in 1890, told us, when she was a young woman, women did not even show their ankles. She was 20 years old in 1910. By the 1920's, the breakthrough for the slow advance of the enemy was the flapper, a straight dress that barely covered the knees and swung loosely so that the tops of her stockings could be "accidentally" seen above the knees when she walked or danced. Young ladies bobbed their hair, and wore short pants to the knees. Now, that is nothing. Shorts to the knee are considered "un-cool". The devil invented being "cool". **"Vanity of vanities; all is vanity." Ecclesiastes 1:2**

One of Crowley's friends near the end of his life was Gerald Gardner, who was initiated into Oriental Templar Orientas (O.T.O.) by Crowley himself, who was the leader of this occult organization in England and Ireland. Gerald Gardner founded the religion of Wicca, which is simply, witchcraft reincarnated for the last days. Several scholars on Wiccan history, such as Ronald Hutton, Philip Heselton and Leo Ruickbie, agree that Wicca's early rituals, as devised by Gardner, contained much from Crowley's writings like the Gnostic Mass.(5) This rebirth of pagan witchcraft, under the harmless sounding name of Wicca, has done much harm. It is America's fastest growing religion, with membership that is doubling every 30 months.(6) The best selling Harry Potter series, based on Wicca teachings, is being consumed by kids and adults alike. I have personally been amazed at the willfully blind eye that parents have turned in letting their children read this series and watch the movies based upon it.

At the end of this book, there is a list of books which you might wish to read to learn more of the roots of the New Age. But one can get a good idea of what Aleister Crowley was thinking and planning by examining a few quotes from some of his writings:

- "I was not content to believe in a personal devil and serve him, in the ordinary sense of the word. I wanted to get hold of him personally and become his chief of staff."
- "Truth! Truth! Truth! Crieth the Lord of the Abyss of Hallucinations" , *The Book of Lies*
- "The most delicious sensation of all is the re-birth of healthy human love. Spring coming back to Earth!", *Diary of a Drug Fiend*
- "Chaos is Peace... Blackness, blackness intolerable, before the beginning of the light. This is the first verse of Genesis. Holy art thou, Chaos, Chaos, Eternity, all contradictions in terms!", *The Vision and the Voice: With Commentary and Other Papers*
- "Magic is nothing but the exercise of willed intent."
- "The key of joy is disobedience."

- "There is no law beyond Do What Thou Wilt!", *The Book of the Law*
- "Astrology has no more useful function than this, to discover the inmost nature of a man and to bring it out into his consciousness, that he may fulfill it according to the law of light.", *The Complete Astrological Writing*
- "I cling unto the burning Æthyr like Lucifer that fell through the Abyss, and by the fury of his flight kindled the air. And I am Belial, for having seen the Rose upon thy breast, I have denied God. And I am Satan! I am Satan! I am cast out upon a burning crag! And the sea boils about the desolation thereof. And already the vultures gather, and feast upon my flesh.", *The Vision and the Voice: With Commentary and Other Paper*
- "Inevitably anyone with an independent mind must become 'one who resists or opposes authority or established conventions': a rebel. If enough people come to agree with, and follow, the Rebel, we now have a Devil. Until, of course, still more people agree. And then, finally, we have – Greatness."
- "Magick is the science and art of causing change to occur in conformity with will.", *Magick in Theory and Practice*
- "Every man and every woman is a star.", *The Book of the Law*
- "Paganism is wholesome because it faces the facts of life...", *The Confessions of Aleister Crowley: An Autohagiograph*
- "Happiness lies within oneself and the way to dig it out is cocaine"

- "Some men are born sodomites, some achieve sodomy, and some have sodomy thrust upon them...", *The Scented Garden Of Abdullah The Satirist Of Shiraz*
- "Love is the law, love under will.", *The Book of the Law*
- "I can imagine myself on my death-bed, spent utterly with lust to touch the next world, like a boy asking for his first kiss from a woman."

And how wrong he was! His death bed quote is below, very revealing were this vile man's last words. Keep reading:

- "I am perplexed" — Aleister Crowley

When Crowley lived, the west was Christian. He was viewed as a perverted rebel. Now people like Aleister Crowley are the norm, and Christians are viewed as the rebels. He died not seeing his satanically inspired words come to fruition; but now they have, and much more. The world in which we live is a much darker place, in part because of the role of Aleister Crowley. Sadly for him, he is in the place he desired to go. "I am perplexed" were his last words. **"It is a fearful thing to fall into the hands of the living God." Hebrews 10:31** We pray that each person who reads this book will not be perplexed, or confused on that day, for **"we must all stand before the Judgment seat of Christ," Romans 10:14**; but that each of your names will be found in the Lamb's Book of Life, so that, as the old gospel song says, "when the roll is called up yonder" you'll be there! When the Lord calls your name, will you be in the Faith doing His work for you? Or will you be like Crowley, perplexed?

Even the wicked Aleister Crowley came from very serious Christian parents. Unbelievably, his parents, who came from modest means, became wealthy, and dedicated their lives to the Gospel. They were a blessing to the body of Christ. Their son chose to serve Satan, even though he knew better. As I often say in my preaching, God has no grandchildren. We must all come to the Lord just as we are; sinners who need His grace and forgiveness. Will you take the words of these apostles of Satan, as a warning? A warning that even very intelligent people can become blinded by the evil they embrace, so that they are unable to hear the truth and be saved? It is called "reprobate" in the Bible, **"And even as they did not like to retain God in their knowledge, God gave them over to a reprobate mind"** **Romans 1:28a**

The Lord no longer calls to those of whom He has washed His hands, for He is finished pleading with them. God forbid that should happen to anyone who would read this book! Let's pray right now, for you, or for our loved ones who are tittering on the edge of the dark pit where these infamous people went.

Heavenly Father,
In the name of Jesus Christ our Lord, have mercy on us (them)! Please extend your hand again Lord! We beseech you just as the gentile woman who approached You, Lord, for healing of her daughter. She pushed past the disciples, who tried to send her away, and kept calling out to you, Lord! She said, "Even the dogs eat crumbs from the Master's table!" You said her faith had

moved your heart to answer her request. We seek, we ask, we knock, LOUDLY! Lord Jesus, save us/our lost family members!

In Jesus' Name we pray.
Amen.

Chapter 3

SATAN'S WORSHIP LEADERS

"But Thou art Holy, O Thou that inhabitest the praises of Israel." Psalm 22:3

G od is the originator of music which He divinely designed out of the overflow of His love for creation. The Bible declares He "sings over us." (Zephaniah 3:17) God Himself sings, and His creation sings also. The book of Job tells us that the sons of God (angels) sang at creation (Job 38:7). The scriptures also proclaim that the Spirit of the Lord inhabits the praises of His people. We know that Jesus sang hymns with His disciples at the Last Supper (Matt. 26:30). And, in a battle to protect Israel, God told King Jehosephat to send singers in front of the army, for the battle was His to win. (2 Chron. 2:20) The Book of Psalms, with 150 chapters, is the biggest book of the Bible and provides some of the oldest evidence that music has always been an important part of worship, an ancient method of praise. The People of God have always used music and song to praise Him.

But music was not just used in worship by God's people, but by ancient pagans as well. Recall that in Daniel 3, Nebuchadnezzar had built a golden statue and set it up on the plain of Dura. When the people heard "sound of the cornet, flute, harp, sackbut, psaltery, dulcimer, and all kinds of music" they were to fall down and worship the golden image. Even in Old Testament times the Enemy was already usurping music for his agenda. Satan, being the Father of Lies and the Master of Deceit, loves to twist God's design into a perverted, evil form, to try and destroy His creation (John 10:9-10).

The Devil comes to steal, to kill and to destroy. He will use any means to achieve his objectives. Such is the case of the modern phenomena of Rock music in which we can see how Satan and his followers are using music to accomplish his goals, to establish the kingdom of Antichrist, and to institute a New World Order.

Satan offered Jesus Christ the kingdoms of this world if He would worship him and Satan is still offering fame and fortune to those who will worship him. One only has to open his eyes to see the corrupting influence of Satan in the music industry. This is not to say that all secular music; even all rock music, is bad. Music is a powerful, emotion evoking medium that can be used for good and noble purposes. Happy tunes can lift one's spirit and mood. Sad songs can do the opposite. Positive, uplifting music is a good and valuable tool. Who does not recall memorizing the alphabet to the tune of "Twinkle Twinkle Little Star?" In the right hands, music can be used for enriching, educational, constructive purposes, as well as for the praise and worship of the One True God. But in the wrong hands, it can be used to release evil. This chapter seeks to discover how secular music has evolved from its beginnings over 60 years ago to the present day, and how Satan uses even music to negatively influence society.

In the 1950's Elvis Presley's dance style shocked American sensibilities and was widely condemned as "a strip-tease with clothes on" and "sexual self-gratification on stage." The general public was horrified by Presley's stage antics that were described as "riding a microphone" because the term "masturbation" made people blush. Psychologists of the day saw Presley as a sexual pervert and feared that teenagers would easily be "aroused to sexual indulgence and perversion by certain types of motions and hysteria,—the type that was exhibited at the Presley show."(7)

Even as late as 1969, when the Doors sang on the Ed Sullivan Show, they were reprimanded for the line, "girl we couldn't get much *higher.*" Because the term "higher" carried the connotation of being intoxicated or "high" on drugs, Ed Sullivan had asked them to alter the lyrics for the live televised performance. Sullivan was concerned about his show's ratings and the backlash from the general public, since "getting high" was a taboo topic for prime time Television 44 years ago.

Fast forward to 2003 and the MTV music awards. Madonna made music history and got a whole lot of press coverage for kissing Britney Spears and Christina Aguilera. But what is hardly mentioned is the fact that the whole performance was a mock lesbian wedding scene with Madonna in a black tuxedo, leather boots and top hat playing the part of the "Groom" and Britney and Christina in their frilly white wedding dresses acting as the "Bride" dancing down the aisle to the traditional wedding march. The kiss was the climax of the song which declared their weariness of the "concept of right and wrong." What was once considered an abomination is now embraced and celebrated by popular culture.

2014, is the 60th anniversary of "Rock Around the Clock" the number one hit single made famous by Bill Haley and His Comets. Their 1954 recording, become an anthem for rebellious youths of the 1950s. It had been written by Max C. Freedman and James E. Myers ("Jimmy De Knight") in 1952; and more than any other song, "Rock Around the Clock" is widely considered to have brought rock and roll music into mainstream culture both in the USA and abroad. *Rolling Stone Magazine* ranks it at #158 on its list of "The 500 Greatest Songs of All Time."[8]

2014 is the 50th anniversary of the "British Invasion." *The Beatles'* song, "I Want to Hold Your Hand," debuted in 1964 and it was the number one, best-selling single that the group ever record. *The Beatles* would go on to become one of rock-and-roll's most influential groups, impacting the music industry for years to come. *The Beatles*, it seems, would also be a microcosm of American Society and its social and moral decline.

The lyrics to "I Want to Hold Your Hand" are an example of innocuous bubble gum rock:

"Oh yeah, I'll tell you something, I think you'll understand…… I want to hold your hand. Oh please, say to me, you'll let me be your man. And please, say to me you'll let me hold your hand. Now let me hold your hand…"

Yet by 1968 and its release of *The White Album*, the Beatles had begun recording songs like "Happiness is a Warm Gun" and "Why Don't We do it in the Road?"

Dr. Howard Hansen, former director of Eastmont School of Music is quoted in the American Journal of Psychiatry, "Music is a curiously subtle art with innumerable varying emotional connotations. It is made up of many ingredients, and according to the proportions of these components, it can be soothing or invigorating, ennobling, or vulgarizing, philosophical or orgiastic. It has powers for evil as well as for good." (9)

But rock n roll did not materialize out of thin air. We need to look at the roots of rock-n-roll to better understand Satan's evil ways; so that we can then anticipate the next move he has planned to further destroy our once-Godly culture.

Rock music stems from four main influences: Country/ folk music, African-influenced soul, rhythm and blues, and jazz. As people began to move into urban areas, once-separate cultures began to influence each other in many ways. Different ethnic groups over-heard each other's music and began to mix musical styles. Rock-and-Roll is the "love child" of that union.(10) One of the earliest nationally known singers was country music star Jimmy Rodgers. Before his music career, Rodgers had been a brakeman for the railroad. His music blended Blues from the Black tradition, time-honored folk tunes, and his own brand of improvised yodeling into a hillbilly style that had wide appeal. His first record, "Blue Yodel #1" was recorded at Trinity Baptist Church in Camden, New Jersey, and became more successful than anyone could ever have predicted.(11) Rodgers career ended in his early death from tuberculosis in 1927.

The 1930s saw Blues-style music becoming well-known and increasingly popular. One of the earliest and most renowned blues singers was Robert Johnson, whose short recording career (1936-1938) earned his entry into the rock and Roll Hall of Fame in their very first induction ceremony and his ranking in the top five "Greatest Guitarists of All Time" by *Rolling Stone*

Magazine. On the 52nd anniversary of his death, *Spin Magazine* rated him first in its "Top 35 Guitar Gods" listing. He has even been called the "Father of Rock and Roll."(12) However, Robert Johnson admitted that he sold his soul to the devil in exchange for fame and guitar playing abilities. Time and retelling of the tale has resulted in varying accounts that all include the struggling blues guitarist walking down a Mississippi road, meeting a tall Black man who borrowed his instrument to tune it and play for him. When the mysterious man returned Johnson's guitar, he received with it the supernatural ability to play like never before. Eric Clapton and Bob Dylan's 1988 song "Crossroads" recounts the legend in song. At the intersection of US Hwy 61 and US Hwy 49 in Clarksdale, Mississippi, the location of this legendary meeting is commemorated by a sign that reads "The Crossroads," topped by larger than life sculptures of blue guitars. Johnson's song, "Me and the Devil" says, "Hello, Satan, I believe it's time to go....You may bury my body down by the highway side, so my old evil spirit can catch a Greyhound bus and ride." Johnson's song, "Hellhound on My Trail" describes a tortured soul who cannot get away from his personal demons. The term "hell hound" is lifted from Black American folklore which uses the term for demonic heralds of death and guardians of the Gates of Hell.

According to David 'Honeyboy' Edwards, the last living witness to the event, the blues legend was poisoned while playing at a dance in Greenwood, Mississippi. Edwards recalled the incident, saying that the person who poisoned Johnson was a jealous lover, "This man had a good-lookin woman and he didn't want to lose her." Edwards states that the man poisoned the pint of corn whiskey Johnson was sipping on as he played guitar, "Robert loved whiskey and women...and some women you got to leave alone, you know what I mean?"(13) He died August 16, 1938, and the mantle of the Father of Rock and Roll would be passed to The King of Rock and Roll.

In the segregated America of 1953, Sun Records executive Sam Phillips was looking for a "white man who had the Negro sound and the Negro feel" to produce records that would have a wide, cross cultural appeal. He found just the man to bridge that gap in Elvis Presley.(14) While still a High School student in Memphis, Tennessee, Elvis debuted on the popular "Red Hot and Blue" radio show with "That's Alright Mama." RCA signed Elvis Presley in1956 for his first record with the hit singles, "Heartbreak Hotel" and "Blue Suede Shoes." The rest, as the saying goes, is history. Elvis would become the "King of Rock and Roll."

What many may not be well-known is Elvis' fascination with the spiritual and the occult. Elvis Presley's twin brother, Jesse, had died at birth. He said many times that he believed his dead brother was with him, guiding him. Elvis' fascination with the paranormal led him to study the book, *The Voice of Silence,* by Madame Helene Blavatsky (1831-1891), the Ukrainian born founder of the Theosophic Society, whose writings introduced eastern (Indian) mysticism and esoteric philosophies to the western world. He even read from this book on stage during performances. Influenced by her writings, Elvis believed that his destiny was directed by the "Brotherhood of Masters" who were illuminated ones or enlightened beings that have existed since before time began, who had chosen him as a modern day "savior." He confided to those who knew him best that be believed he had a mission to use his voice as a "channel" to introduce the masses to the "Spiritual World" through "the universal language of music."(15) All of his study of mystic teachings and ancient philosophies did not bring peace of mind to the "King of Rock." It did produce an obsession with the after-life. In his book, *Elvis: What Happened?,* Steve Dunleavy, states that Elvis Presley became so obsessed with death that he would have his body guards take him to graveyards and funeral homes as late as three o'clock in the morning, where Elvis would "wander about the slabs looking at all the embalmed bodies."(16) He confided to Pastor James E. Haffmill of Memphis First Assembly of God that in spite of all of his wealth and fame, he was a miserable man. Elvis Presley died August 16, 1977, exactly 39 years to the day after the poisoning death of Blues legend, Robert Johnson. Elvis was poisoned, too, in a manner of speaking. His autopsy revealed 14 different drugs in his system, so many that some have questioned whether his death was an overdose or a suicide.

The life of Richard Wayne Penniman, aka, Little Richard, tells the story of rock-n-roll: sex, drugs, and Satan. In 1955, producer Robert 'Bumps' Blackwell, heard Little Richard perform "Tutti Frutti" live and knew it could be a hit. But he also knew that it had to be cleaned up for radio play. The original lyrics, "Tutti Frutti, good booty, If it don't fit, don't force it, You can grease it, make it easy," were replaced with "Tutti Frutti, aw rooty! Tutti Frutti, aw rooty". They recorded "Tutti Frutti" in Sept 1955 and by November of that same year it was #2 on the *Billboard Rhythm and Blues* charts. Little Richard was almost as popular as Elvis by the end of the decade (1950s).(17) In 1956, Little Richard, who admits to having voyeuristic tendencies, was arrested in Macon, Georgia along with another man and a woman who were having sex in the back seat of a car at a gas station while

Little Richard watched. He spent three days in a Macon jail and was temporarily banned from performing in that town.(18) Little Richard also admits to an extreme drug habit (though he now claims to be clean) and in one interview said, "They shoulda called me Little Cocaine, I was sniffing so much of the stuff! My nose got big enough to back a diesel truck in, unload it, and drive it right out again."(19) In another interview, Little Richard credits Satan as his source of inspiration: "I was directed and commanded by another power, the power of darkness...that a lot of people don't believe exists. The power of the devil. Satan."

By 1967, the work of Aleister Crowley had become a great influence in the life of one of the most prolific Beatles songwriters, John Lennon. The *Sergeant Pepper's Lonely Hearts Club* album was released 20 years after Crowley's death, and the words to the title song reveal that this album was meant as an anniversary tribute to him: "It was twenty years ago today, Sgt. Pepper taught the band to play..."(20) The cover of *Sergeant Pepper's Lonely Hearts Club* Album depicts some sixty-seven different people standing behind the four Beetles band members. The second person from the left on the back row is Aleister Crowley. Standing to his left is the Indian Guru, Sri Yukteswar Gigi. In front of the 67 people, there are 21 different objects, including a four-armed Indian doll, a representation of the goddess Lakshmi. Lakshmi is the goddess of material and spiritual wealth and prosperity. Its name comes from the Sanskrit, "Laksme", which means "goal." Thus, Lakshmi represents the goal of life for Hindus: worldly prosperity and spiritual enlightenment.

Sgt. Pepper's Lonely Hearts Club Band contained the song, "Lucy in the Sky with Diamonds." Because the initials of the title are "L.S.D.", soon after its release, speculation began that the song was about the illegal hallucinogen drug. In fact the BBC actually banned the song from British radio at the time. In a 2004 Weekly Standard interview, Paul McCartney not only admitted that this song was about LSD, but that several other Beatles songs were actually about the use of illegal drugs. "A song like 'Got to Get You Into My Life,' that's directly about pot, although everyone missed it at the time." "Day Tripper," he says, "that's one about acid. 'Lucy in the Sky,' that's pretty obvious. There's others that make subtle hints about drugs, but, you know, it's easy to overestimate the influence of drugs on the Beatles' Music." [21] "Lucy in the Sky with Diamonds" has since become a classic in the "psychedelic rock" music, a classification of music that began in the 1960s which attempts to replicate in sound and lyrics the experience of being high on mind-altering drugs like LSD.

The Beatles is considered to be one of the "pioneering" psychedelic rock bands not only because of songs like "Lucy in the Skye with Diamonds" but also because of its incorporation of non-western, especially Indian, sound, rhythm and instrumentation. It was a band on the cutting edge of the New Age Movement. The term *New Age* refers to the coming astrological Age of Aquarius. The central precepts of the New Age Movement "draw on both Eastern and Western spiritual and metaphysical traditions and infuses them with influences from self-help and motivational psychology, holistic health, parapsychology, consciousness research and quantum physics." [22]

The lyrics to "Image", by John Lennon, illustrate the Beatles embrace of the idea of the New Age of enlightenment, a New World Order:

"Imagine there's no heaven. It's easy if you try. No hell below us. Above us only sky. Imagine all the people Living for today... Imagine there's no countries. It isn't hard to do. Nothing to kill or die for. And no religion too. Imagine all the people Living life in peace... You may say I'm a dreamer But I'm not the only one. I hope someday you'll join us and the world will be as one."

Timothy Leary once said that the Beatles are like "Listening to the Beatles album is like an hour of de-conditioning." It could be put another way, depending upon one's view point: "Listening to the Beatles album is like an hour of indoctrination."

Something strange, it seems, was happening with the music produced by the Beatles. John Lennon of the Beetles told People Magazine that the tune to "In My Life" came to him in a dream.(23) Paul McCartney said the same thing about the music to "Yesterday", "[it] came in a dream. The tune just came complete. You have to believe in magic. I can't read or write music."(24) Yoko Ono told Playboy Magazine that the Beetles "were like mediums. They weren't even conscious of what they were saying, but it was coming through them."(25)

The Beach Boys formed in 1961 with the three Wilson brothers, Brian Dennis, and Carl, and friends Mike Love and Al Jardene, reached its height of popularity 1964-1973. Brian Wilson's creativity and songwriting skills dominated the group's musical direction with songs like "Good Vibrations," "Surfin' Safari," and "Do You Want to Dance." But, the stress of travel schedules, songwriting, and production deadlines was too much for Brian, who soon turned to drinking and drug use in an effort to cope. Brain was tortured by distracting voices in his head that tormented him. In his interview for *Rolling Stone Magazine* (Nov. 4, 1976 issue), David Felton records, "Brian Wilson hears voices.

They talk to him. They distract him, frighten him, confuse him." Warner Brothers Records president, Larry Waronker, claimed to have had interaction with at least five different personalities, or entities, in Brian Wilson.(26) But voices in Brian's head would not be the only evil force the Beach Boys would encounter.

In 1968, Dennis Wilson of the *Beach Boys* struck up a friendship with a struggling musician named Charles Manson, letting him live in his Bel Air home for some months. During that time, Wilson tried to help Manson in his musical career by recording one of Manson's songs, "Cease to Exist." Wilson reworked the words to fit the *Beach Boys'* style, changing the line "cease to exist" to "cease to resist", and altering the title of the song to "Never Learn Not to Love". In September 1968, *The Beach Boys* recorded Manson's song in their studio in Bel Air, California and it was released in December 1968 on side-B of their "Bluebirds over the Mountains" single from the album *20/20*. Manson was reportedly furious that his lyrics had been changed and came to Wilson's home, threatening him with murder. Dennis Wilson beat up Charles Manson, and everyone thought that was the end.(27)

During the time that Manson lived with Dennis Wilson, he had been given one of *The Beach Boys'* gold records as a souvenir. When they parted ways, Manson convinced the elderly woman who owned Barker ranch that he and his friends were musicians, gave her the Beach Boys' gold record which he had received from Dennis Wilson, and told her they would fix up the ranch if she let them stay. While hiding out, Manson heard the *Beatles'* White Album, and became convinced that the song "Helter Skelter" was really a secret code—a prophecy—of a coming race war. He persuaded his followers that when the blacks had killed the whites, Manson and his "Family" would come out of hiding to rule America.(28) He planned to incite this race war, "Helter Skelter", by murdering prominent people and making it look like Black on White crime.

Charles Manson and his followers were convicted for the murder of 9 people: Leno and Rosemary LaBianca, a wealthy couple who owned a supermarket chain, actress Sharon Tate, who was eight months pregnant, as well as her six houseguests who were visiting her at the time of the vicious attack the night of August 8, and into the early morning hours of August 9, 1969. All of the victims were stabbed multiple times. With the blood of his victims, Manson wrote the words "Helter Skelter" on the walls of the crime scenes, the title of the song from *The Beatles'* "White" album which had inspired him.

Jimi Hendrix's 1967 album "Are You Experienced" became a double-platinum and is ranked by Rolling Stone as the 15th greatest albums of all-time. Rolling Stone described Hendrix's guitar playing as "incendiary ... historic in itself" and the album as an "epoch debut."(29) It spent 33 weeks on the charts, peaking at number 2 in the U.K. Some would argue that Jimi Hendrix was rock's greatest guitarist, and he is admitted to be the Father of Heavy Metal. But he believed that something supernatural was controlling him. Hendrix's former girlfriend, Fayne Prigdon, said, "He used to always talk about some devil or something was in him, you know, and he didn't have any control over it. He didn't know what made him act the way he acted and what made him say the things he said, and the songs…just come out of him."(30) Hendrix died in 1970 in London at age 27; intoxicated with sleeping pills, he was suffocated when he choked on his own vomit.

1967 also saw the release of *The Doors,* a self-titled album from one of the most controversial rock bands of the time. The Doors, the band, got its name from Aldous Huxley's book, *The Doors of Perception,*(30) Their lead singer was Jim Morrison had left UCLA in 1965 and moved to Venice Beach. In the book, *Break on Through: The Life and Death of Jim Morrison,* he is quoted as saying, "I left school and went down to the beach to live. I slept on a roof….I met the Spirit of Music, an appearance of the Devil on a Venice canal, running. I saw Satan." Morrison's drinking and drug use opened a "door" to the spiritual realm. He began hearing voices that downloaded songs into his head. Of his songwriting on Venice Beach, Morrison said, "I was just taking notes at a fantastic rock concert that was going on inside my head."(31) The title of the first song on The Doors' first album is "Break on Through (to the Other Side)" Morrison received so much "inspiration" communicated to him that his Venice Beach song-writing period was prolific enough for two albums in 1967, *The Doors* and *Strange Days,* critically acclaimed as *The Doors'* best work.

But Jim Morrison's artistic inspirations did not bring him peace; quite the opposite. Franck Lisciandro, the *Doors'* photographer and close friend of Morrison said, "Jim drank…to quiet the ceaseless clamor of demons, ghosts and spirits begging to be released. He drank because there were demons and voices and spirits shouting inside his head, and he found one of the ways to quell them was from alcohol."(32) On December 9, 1967, after an obscenity-laden tirade to his concert audience in New Haven Arena, New Haven, Connecticut, the *Doors'* performance was abruptly ended with Morrison being dragged off stage by police and arrested for inciting a riot, indecency and public obscenity. This was only the beginning. 1968 saw multiple clashes between police and *The Doors* concert-goers. Then on March 1, 1969, in the Coconut Grove neighborhood of Miami, Florida, Jim Morrison's performance almost ended the band's career. The clearly intoxicated lead singer began taunting the crowd with "I want some lovin'. Ain't nobody gonna love my ass?" and You're all a bunch of f_ckin' idiots!" Then, someone opened a champaign bottle which spewed onto Morrison's shirt, soaking it. He took off the shirt and screamed "Let's see a little skin, let's get naked!" At which suggestion, the audience began taking their clothes off. During this scene, Morrison put his wet shirt over his groin and began to masturbate on the stage.(33)

The March 5, 1969, Dade County Sheriff's official arrest warrant sited public drunkenness, deliberate exposition of his private parts, shouting obscenities and simulating oral sex on guitarist Robby Kriegar. Morrison refused the plea bargain offered, and ended up sentenced to six months in jail, with hard labor, and a $500 fine. He remained free while appealing the case and would be deceased before the issue was resolved.(34)

On July 3, 1971, Jim Morrison was found dead in a Paris apartment bathtub. The medical examiner indicated that there was no evidence of foul play; so under French law, an autopsy did not have to be performed.(35) Jim Morrison had opened himself up to be "used and abused by any spiritual entity that happened to come along." In so doing, he may have received some amazing songwriting inspiration, but he also fell into a tragically destructive lifestyle which resulted in his premature death at only 27 years old.(36)

Carlos Santana, whose band, *Santana,* bears his name, played live at Woodstock in 1969. It was this performance which launched the group into its height of success. Santana, who was high on LSD during his Woodstock act, claims to have channeled a spirit for his musical inspiration. When recalling the event, he said that his guitar became a serpent right before his very eyes, and was responsible for his brilliant playing.(37) Since 1994, Santana has claimed to be in regular communication with an "angel" whose name is Metatron. He connects to the spirit of Metatron via meditation. "...You meditate and you got the candles, you got the incense and you're chanting, and all of a sudden you hear this voice: 'Write this down'."(38) He asserts that Metatron uses his music and the band, *Santana* to get people in touch with their own divinity.

The Rolling Stones Album, *Beggars Banquet,* with its single "Sympathy for the Devil," was released in 1968. Though it may be hard to believe now, it did stir quite some controversy among music listeners at the time. It was groundbreaking new subject matter for mainstream Rock and Roll, and it was a game changer for radio played lyrics in that it opened the door for direct expression of a growing fascination with evil.

> "Please allow me to introduce myself I'm a man
> of wealth and taste. I've been around for a long,
> long year, stole many a man's soul and faith. And
> I was round when Jesus Christ had his moment
> of doubt and pain. Made damn sure that Pilate
> washed his hands and sealed his fate. Pleased
> to meet you, hope you get my name...."

In 1969, Geezer Butler, bass guitarist for the group *Black Sabbath,* and Ozzie Osbourne wrote a song entitled "Black

Sabbath." Robert Halford of *Judas Priest* (who calls himself "Lord Lucifer", and is credited for being the first openly gay heavy metal musician(39) said that the song "Black Sabbath" was "probably the most evil song ever written." This song was the inspiration for the band from Birmingham, England (which formerly played blues and polka) to change its name and its sound. Occult themes with horror-inspired lyrics and dark and disturbing stage performances became the order of the day. During Black Sabbath concerts of the 1970s and 80s, Ozzie Osbourne famously bit the heads off of bats and doves, and gave "altar calls" inviting concert goers to come to Satan. Ozzie Osbourne said of his stage antics, "I never seem to know exactly what I'm gonna do next. I just like to do what the spirits make me do. That way, I always have someone or something to blame."(40) Bill Ward of Black Sabbath said, "I've always considered that there was some way where we were able to channel energy, and that energy was able to be from another source, if you like, like a higher power or something, that was actually doing the work. I've often thought of us just being actually just the earthly beings that played the music because it was uncanny. Some of this music came out extremely uncanny."(41)Black Sabbath produced albums with titles like "Sabbath, Bloody Sabbath", "Sabotage", "Heaven & Hell", "Mob Rules", "Headless Cross" and "Dehumanizer ", to mention just a few, reinforcing their blasphemous song lyrics and violent concert behavior.

The song, "Suicide Solution" from Ozzie Osbourne's 1980 album, *Blizzard of Oz*, glorifies suicide as an alternative to a disappointing life:

"sick of life, it sucks, sick and tired, no one cares,
sick of myself, don't wanna live, sick o living,
gonna die, suicides an alternative....wine is fine,
but whiskey's quicker, Suicide is slow with liquor."

Sadly, in 1990, the national Education Association conducted a study which concluded that nihilistic and fatalistic music contributes to 6000 teen suicides every year.(42 The medieval fairy tale, *The Pied Piper of Hamelin*, tells the story of a traveling minstrel who proposed to cure the town of Hamelin of its rat infestation by playing his pipe. When he had rid the town of rats, the mayor cast him out of the town without paying him the amount promised. The piper returned some time later to exact his revenge, playing his music to lure away the children of the village who were never to be seen again. This poignantly illustrates how Satan uses music. Seeking revenge upon God for casting him out of Heaven, Satan is using music to lure God's children to Hell.

In October 1970, Jimmy Paige of the Rock band, *Led Zeppelin,* rented the sprawling farmhouse on Loch Ness (of monster fame) which had been the home of Aleister Crowley. Crowley had purchased the home because its secluded location was perfect for him to perform the extensive black magic rituals which he had read about in *The Book of the Sacred Magic of Abramelin the Mage.*(43) Evil spirits were unleashed during the 6-month long black magic rituals which would reemerge for Led Zeppelin approximately 60 years later when Jimmy Paige and the band members came to the Crowley house in an attempt to channel his spirit to help them write a hit song. The result was "Stairway to Heaven." In an interview with band member,

Robert Plant, he states, "Pagey [Jimmy Paige] had written some chords and played them for me. I was holding the paper and pencil... then all of a sudden my hand was writing out words... I just sat there and looked at the words and almost leaped out of my seat!"(44)

The phenomenon Robert Plant describes is termed "automatic writing." Those in the paranormal community describe this experience as a ghost or entity using a person as a channel to express the message that the entity wants to convey without the writer's conscious awareness of the content. Spiritualists who practice this say they passively hold pencil to paper and allow themselves to be the medium through which the entity expresses its written message.

In 1982, a prominent Baptist minister played "Stairway to Heaven" backward on his radio show to illustrate that there were subliminal messages masked in the song. He argued that even though the messages are not perceived by the conscious mind when listening to the song played forward, that our subconscious is absorbing these messages hidden in the backward lyrics. This type of subliminal suggestion is said to influence the thoughts and actions of the listener. The controversy grew to the point that in April 1982, the California State Assembly played a backward tape of the song in a public session.

The second stanza of the song contains the words "words have two meanings" and "thoughts are misgiven." When this section of the recording is played backward, it seems to say, "Plaaaaaay back ward." Other portions of the song seem to reverse to "There's no escaping it, I will sing 'cause I live with Satan" and the last stanza seems to reverse to. "It's my sweet Satan, whose little path will make me sad."

Everyone in the band has denied any deliberate attempt to insert subliminal messages into the song via backward masking. Eddie Kramer, producer of the untitled album often referred to as "Led Zeppelin IV," said of the charges of "Stairway to Heaven" backward masking, "[they are] totally and utterly ridiculous! Why would they want to spend so much studio time doing something so dumb?" Eddie Kramer is correct. They did not spend studio time encoding backward messages because these same messages can be heard in the live version of "Stairway to Heaven."(45)

Perhaps in the course of writing the song, Robert Plant unknowingly established the vocal criteria for reversals to occur within the lyrics. That would be a remarkable coincidence. What are the odds of *accidentally* encoding recognizable backwards speech within a song? Could it be that the same entity that enabled the writing of the song without conscious effort on his part, also encoded the backward messages? This possibility points to something paranormal taking place in the writing and recording of "Stairway to Heaven," something of demonic origin.

Robert Pant, having admitted that some otherworldly influence helped him to write the song, "Stairway to Heaven", coupled with the documented evidence before the California State Assembly that hidden messages encoded in the song are revealed when it is played backward, point toward an evil influence at work. By 1975, Led Zepplin's references to Satan were no longer masked backward, but spoken forward. In the song, "Houses of the Holy" from the group's *Physical Graffiti* album, they say, "Let the music be your master. Won't you heed the master's call? Oh, Satan!"

Robert Plant's experience of an outside force influencing song lyrics or Santana's feeling that he was channeling spirits during his Woodstock performance are not an isolated events. Angus Young lead guitarist of AC-DC said, "…It's like I'm on automatic pilot. By the time we're halfway through the first number, someone else is steering me…I'm just along for the ride. I become possessed when I get on stage."(46)

The AC-DC song, "Night Prowler" tells the story of someone sneaking out at night for sex. Laced with violence, one of its verses says, "No one's gonna warn you, no one's gonna yell 'attack!' and you can't feel the steel until it's hanging out your back, I'm your night prowler." Inspired by the song, "Night Prowler", serial killer, Richard Ramirez, a native of El Paso, Texas, called himself "The Night Stalker." This notorious criminal's convictions include 13 counts of murder, 5 attempted murders, 11 sexual assaults and 14 burglaries. His victims range in age from the 9 year old Mei Lueng whose body was found in the basement of the hotel in which Ramirez was living at the time, to 83 year old Malvia Keller, whom he beat to death with a hammer.(47)

The Rolling Stones had cracked open the door to the Satan with "Sympathy for the Devil" and blasphemies have rushed in through that open door. What was begun by rock and roll legends like *The Rolling Stones, Judas Priest,* and *Black Sabbath,* have been continued and expanded upon by bands that would follow in their footsteps. Such groups would openly embrace the occult as illustrated by their band's names and their song's lyrics: *Dark Angel, Demon, Infernal Majesty, Possessed, Satan,* and *Cloven Hoof*, to name but a few. *Skid Row*'s "Quicksand Jesus" asks, "Are we saved by the words of bastard saints?" "The Oath" by *King Diamond* declares, "I deny Jesus Christ, the deceiver, and I adjure the Christian faith, holding in contempt all of its works." The song, "Possessed" by Venom says, "I am possessed by all that is evil. The death of your God I demand. I …sit at Lord Satan's right hand…I drink the vomit of the priest, make love to the dying whore, Satan is my master incarnate, hail, praise to my unholy host!" "Hymn 43" from the band, *Jethro Tull,* declares, "We are our own saviors, and if Jesus saves, then He better save Himself."(48)

Michael Jackson, the "King of Pop," was the most popular musician of the 1980's and beyond. He received thirty-one Guinness Book of World Records awards including 1984 Best Selling Album of all Time for "Thriller", 1986 Most Successful Concert Series for *Bad* World Tour. 1993 Largest Entertainment Contract Ever ($890 million) with Sony Music, 2002 Best Selling Music Video for "The Making of Thriller", 2006 Most Weeks at the Top of the US Album Charts for Thriller, 2006 First Vocalist to Enter the US Single Chart at Number One for "You are Not Alone", and 2009, the year of his death, Longest Span of No.1 Hits by an R&B Artist. Since his death on June 25, 2009, he has made the Guinness Book of World Records for "Highest Earning Deceased Artist" in 2010, and "Longest Span of US top-40 Singles" in 2011. When *Rolling Stone Magazine* asked Michael Jackson about his song-writing inspiration, in 1983, he said, "I wake up from dreams and go 'Wow, put that down on paper!' The whole thing is strange. You hear words, everything is right there in front of your face. I feel that somewhere, someplace it's been done and I'm just a courier bringing it into the world."(49)

Michael Jackson also studied the works of Aleister Crowley. "The Moonwalk" made world-famous by Michael Jackson, was inspired by "The Book of the Law" by Aleister Crowley, who claimed it to have taken only one hour to write each chapter as it did not come from his own imagination but had been dictated to him by his angel, Aiwess.(50) This book recommended practicing speaking, reading and walking backward. Jackson perfected backward walking, first performing his "moonwalk" in1983 at the Motown 25 Celebration, and made it his trademark dance move by incorporating it into every performance of his career. (51) For all his fame and acclaim, Michael Jackson was a tormented soul. In a CNN interview shortly after his death in 2009, Rabbi Schmuley Boteach, speaking with Campbell Brown said, "Michael always thought he had ailments of the body...Really, he had an affliction of his soul. He was extremely lonely, he was extremely unhappy. He felt purposeless, he felt lethargic....and he decided to medicate away his pain...I think Michael lived with a profound fear of rejection. And Michael told me once—and this was a heartbreaking conversation between us—'Shmuley, I promise I'm not lying to you,' he said. 'I'm not lying to you.' He said that twice. 'But everything I've done in pursuing fame, in honing my craft' to quote his words, 'was an effort to be loved because I never felt loved.' And he used to say that to me all the time. And you can image if you're trying to get love from the crowd and you're not sure how they're going to react to you because time is going on, they [call you] "Wacko-jacko"—you've become a tabloid caricature. You live in phenomenal fear. And I think...the prescription drugs were used to address and alleviate the anxiety. And it was just tragic to watch."

Dr. Conrad Murray, Michael Jackson's physician, was found guilty of involuntary manslaughter on November 7, 2011 and sentenced to four years in jail. Just like Robert Johnson, Elvis Presley, Jimi Hendrix, Jim Morrison, and countless others, the deception of drugs had destroyed Michael Jackson as well. Satan is not merciful and longsuffering like God. He wants all to perish and none to come to repentance. The Devil wants to drag as many souls into Hell with him as he possibly can. He promises his followers fortune, fame, power, pleasure. But he fails to inform those he has enticed that when they are at their lowest and most venerable, he will snuff out their lives and take their souls.

Whether the influence is subtle or overt, many rock-n-roll artists have admitted to otherworldly guidance in composing and performing their music, some even openly acknowledge selling their soul to the devil in exchange for success in the music industry.

Singer, Marc Storace, of the heavy-metal band *Krokus*, in a *Circus Magazine* interview, said of his performances, "You can't describe it except to say it's like a mysterious energy that comes from the metaphysical plane and into my body. It's almost like being a medium."

David Bowie is another artist who claims to be aided by a supernatural force in his songwriting and performances. His rock-god alter ego is called "Ziggy Stardust." Ziggy Stardust spoke to Bowie of peace and love while leading him into sexual promiscuity, wild drug use, and general excess.(52) David Bowie told Rolling Stone Magazine, "Rock has always been the devil's music; you can't convince me that it isn't. I honestly believe everything I've said—I believe rock and roll is dangerous....I feel that we're only heralding something even darker than ourselves."(53)

Tori Amos, alternative-New Age singer-songwriter, once said, "I think music comes through dimensions, it's arrogant to think you can create music on your own...there is this well that we all tap into," and, "I want to marry Lucifer. I don't consider Lucifer an evil force. I feel his presence with his music. I feel like he comes and sits on my piano."(54)

Rapper, Eminem also claims to be possessed by an entity called "Slim Shady" which inspires his rap lyrics about rape, murder and gore. Eminem, who struggles with drug addiction, says that Slim Shady is the dark, evil, creatively sick side of himself, the one who thinks and says things that Eminem himself would never think or say. He says of his introduction to Slim Shady, "Slim Shady was coming to haunt me, was coming to haunt Eminem."(55)

And then there is Beyonce Knowles. *Rolling Stone Magazine's* cover story posted March 4, 2004 read, "A Woman Possessed: Beyonce is gripped by a spirit so powerful it even has a name—Sasha!" Beyonce Knowles admits to her fans that "Sasha Fierce was born when I did *Crazy in Love*." She says, too, that when she is "in the moment," when Sasha is performing, she (Beyonce) cannot even remember what goes through her mind.(56) In her interview with BET, April 2006, Beyonce said, "Sometimes I think that when they [fans] meet me and they speak to me, they're expecting Sasha; and, I'm really kind of shy, more reserved, nothing like Sasha. But, I guess I wouldn't be very entertaining on the stage, so Sasha comes out. And she's fearless! She can do things that I cannot do in rehearsal. I mean, I can try, but it just doesn't happen....[with Sasha] I can sing notes and sing strong that when I'm by myself I just cannot do...I remember that right before I performed, I raised my hands up and it was kind of the first time I *felt* something else come into me, and I *knew* that was gonna be my coming out night."

Heavy metal vocalist, Marilyn Manson (Brian Hugh Warner), who created his stage name by combining "Marilyn Monroe" and "Charles Manson", is a Satanist, a member of The Church of Satan started by Anton LeVey. It is interesting that he chose a stage name that combines both male and female identities. Marilyn Manson has appeared in some of his performances wearing breasts, like Baphomet, the mythological figure adopted as the symbol of Satanists.

The nineteenth century image of Baphomet depicts him as a winged goat, seated cross-legged, having three horns—the middle horn being shaped roughly like a fleur de lis— a five-pointed star (pentagram) on his forehead and breasts like a woman. Rising from between his crossed legs, almost as a phallic symbol, is a pole with two snakes twisted around it, facing each other similar to the staff often depicted in the left hand of the Roman god Mercury, patron of commerce and communication. The Baphomet symbol, with one arm extended down and the other pointing up, is meant to represent the duality of the cosmos: male and female, night and day, Heaven and Hell, good and evil. (57)

Speaking of his fascination with the Satan and the Antichrist, Marilyn Manson said, "since I was about sixteen, I've had really intense dreams...and in my dreams I'd always be trying to find out who [the Antichrist] was going to be. Then at one point I saw myself....So I hope that each time [my album] "Antichrist" is played, it brings people closer to the end of the world...." Manson's concerts are dark and disturbing, which is exactly what he intends. "The concert is satanic. Just by being in the audience, you are entering my own personal satanic ritual." Of his audience, he said that they "don't know whether to f- ck each other or kill each other, and hopefully, the same goes for listening to the record."(58) He admittedly uses music as a means of indoctrination of his audience, "I incorporate satanic philosophy, more times subtly than others. It gets across the philosophy without the name 'Satanism.' After people get close to me, I let them know my affiliation with the church [of Satan]."(59)

Not only is Rock music laced with occult practices and spiritualism, but it is saturated with sex. American philosopher and academic, Allen Bloom, correctly said, "rock music has one appeal only, a barbaric appeal, to the sexual desires—not love...but sexual desire undeveloped and untutored...rock gives children, on a silver plate, with all the public authority of the entertainment industry, everything their parents always used to tell them they had to wait for until they grew up...Young people know that rock has the beat of sexual intercourse...The words implicitly and explicitly describe bodily acts that satisfy sexual desire and treat them as its only natural and routine culmination for children who do not yet have the slightest imagination of love, marriage or family."(60) From "Sexual Healing" by the late Marvin Gay to George Michael's "I Want Your Sex," Rock and roll music has always had a sexual theme. In fact the term "rock and roll" originally referred to the type of cadence or beat of music that mimics the rhythm of sexual intercourse. Song lyrics with subject matter of lust, infidelity, fornication, sadism, masochism, homosexuality, rape, even necrophilia abound.

Subject matter that was once marketed to adult consumers is now being pedaled to elementary-school-age children. The

British all-girl band, Spice Girls, is one such group which has a mostly pre-adolescent fan base. "Get Down with Me" from its 2000 album, *Forever,* is one example of sexually graphic lyrics now offered to our youth:

> "Now that we have been together for a night (now that, together for a night), It's time that you and I to say goodbye (it's time, say goodbye) Don't try to hold on to this moment (to hold on to this moment), Cos when you wake up I'll be gone, yeah, yeah-yeah, If you knew (if you knew) Just what plan I has got in store for you (ah, just what the night has got in store), You wouldn't leave the room until I am through (til I am through, no-no, no), I'm tired of being undercover (I don't wanna be), It's time to be your lover (now it's time to be), So get down with me"

According to *National Geographic*, hip hop is "the world's favorite youth culture," and "just about every country on the planet seems to have developed its own local rap scene. In this age of international travel, hip hop has become a global music phenomenon.(61) Rapping is a vocal style that was first used in hip hop music in the late 1980's and has since found its way into every genre of music from Gospel to Rock, Country to Pop. Sometimes called MC-ing (emceeing), the artist speaks in rhyme or verse, sometimes a cappella, but most often to the rhythm of an instrumental or synthesized background beat.

MC Hammer was one of the first rappers to be embraced by main-stream music consumers with his 1990 hit single, "U Can't

Touch This" from his album, *Please Hammer, Don't Hurt 'Em.* It had catchy lyrics and a happy beat: "Can't touch this, Can't touch this, Can't touch this. My, my, my music hits me so hard, Makes me say 'Oh my Lord', Thank You for blessing me, With a mind to rhyme and two hype feet." But, MC Hammer is no longer performing and rap, after starting out innocently enough, has gone the way of its predecessor Rock and Roll—from benign, to bad, to worse.

Hispanic hip-hop artist and rapper, Pitbull's single "I Know You Want Me (Calle Ocho)" was released in 2009 and hit the Billboard 100 at number 2 that year. The characteristically catchy rap rhythms are there, but gone is the happy innocence of "Can't Touch This." Rather, these are its lyrics in part:

"One, two, three, four! Uno, dos, tres, cuatro!
Baby you can get it, if you with it we can play,
Baby I got cribs,
I got condos we can stay. Even got a king size
mattress we can lay.
Baby I don't care, I don't care, what they say..."

Nicki Manaj's album *Pink Friday* (2010) reached number 1 on the U.S. *Billboard* 200 and was Platinum (sold 1 Million copies) only one month after its release. She made history as the first American female artist to have seven songs in Billboard's top 100 at the same time.(62) Her second album, *Pink Friday: Roman Reload,* contained the hit single, "Va Va Voom", a song which extols adultery. A portion of the lyrics is as follows:

"….Boom boom pow, this thing be shakin', I ain't even tryin' to find out who he datin', Cause I know that he got a wife at home, But I need just one night alone, If he keep playing them kiddin' games, I'm a runaway-eh, I'm a runaway-eh-eh, I-I-I wanna give you one last option, I-I-I wanna give you one last chance, If-if you're looking for the main attraction, Just hold on tight and let me do my dance…"

The sexual content of rap music is only eclipsed by its violence. So graphically violent are some of its lyrics that politicians and activists have joined together in protest of some of the most violent rap. The late C. Delores Tucker, a civil rights activist who marched in the famous civil rights demonstrations in Selma, Alabama in the 1960s, devoted countless hours circulating petitions, picketing music stores, even using her own retirement savings to buy stock in music companies so that she could attend shareholder's meetings and make her case with the boards of directors against the violence of "Gangsta Rap."(63)

Rapper Notorious B.I.G.'s final album was released 16 days after he was killed by a drive-by shooter on March 9, 1997 and it swiftly skyrocketed to number one on the Billboard 100. By 2000, over 10 Million copies had been sold. The song "Hypnotize" from that album which was nominated for a Grammy, contains the following lyrics:

"them niggas ride dicks, Frank White push the sticks on the Lexus, LX, four and a half, Bulletproof glass tints if I want some ass. Gonna

86

blast , squeeze first ask questions last. That's how most of these so-called gangsters pass. At last, a nigga rappin 'bout blunts and broads, tits and bras, ménage a trios, sex in expensive cars, I still leave you on the pavement. Condo paid for, no car payment. At my arraignment, note for the plaintiff, Your daughter's tied up in a Brooklyn basement..."(64)

Getto Boys' 2008 album *We Can't be Stopped* contains so many controversial and violent lyrics that Sony refused to release it as originally recorded.(65) It's song, "Gotta Let 'em Hang" talks about drug dealers killing police officers,

"Pretend to be lawmen, and come out with dope,
But first we gotta find a bitch with nuts, A down-ass bitch, who doesn't give a f-ck
Distracts the cops, on duty, Walkin around shakin nothin but booty
That's when we make our motion...First we'll hit 'em up with some gas
Then launch a missle on they mother f- ckin ass....
You wanna get paid mayne? Well that's what you gotta do; and you better let your nuts hang! You gotta let your nuts hang... ha ha!"

But thou art holy, O Thou that inhabitest the praises of Israel. Psalm 22:3

Psalm 22:3 is rendered in the NIV footnotes as "But You are holy, enthroned in the praises of Israel." This translation of the KJV word "inhabits" strengthens the concept. God inhabits (lives in) the praises of His people. God is *enthroned* (reigns as sovereign, is exalted) in the praises of his people. **Likewise Satan inhabits the praises of his people, too.** When music exalts evil and sin, even Satan himself, he is getting exactly what he has always wanted, WORSHIP.

Isaiah 14:13-14, "For thou hast said in thine heart, I will ascend into heaven, I will exalt my throne above the stars of God: I will sit also upon the mount of the congregation, in the sides of the north: I will ascend above the heights of the clouds; I will be like the most High."

John Lennon said, "Christianity will go. It will vanish and shrink. I needn't argue with that; I'm right and I will be proved right. We're more popular than Jesus now; I don't know which will go first–rock and roll or Christianity."

People see the world through the very narrow window of time, and more specifically, their own time. Even though today Rock music seems big, compare it to music from other ages. Do you know any famous musicians from the 1500's? Do you know the father of the Atomic bomb? Do you know who discovered DNA? There are many young people today, who do not even know who John Lennon is. His influence is much less than Julius Robert Oppenheimer; who invented the atomic bomb, or Watson and Crick, the team who mapped DNA as a double helix for the first time.

The Bible reminds us in James 4:13-14, **"Go to now, ye that say, To day or to morrow we will go into such a city,** and continue there a year, and buy and sell, and get gain: Whereas ye know not what *shall be* on the morrow. For what *is* your life? It is even a vapour, that appeareth for a little time, and then vanisheth away."

Philippians 2:10-11 tells us that one day, **"every knee should bow, of things in heaven, and things in earth, and things under the earth; And that every tongue should confess that Jesus Christ is Lord, to the glory of God the Father."**

Even John Lennon, will confess—with that same tongue he used to declare *The Beatles* more popular than Jesus, and "Christianity would go"—that Jesus Christ is Lord, at the Great White Throne Judgment.

Revelation 20:11-14, "And I saw a great white throne, and him that sat on it, from whose face the earth and the heaven fled away; and there was found no place for them. And I saw the dead, small and great, stand before God; and the books were opened: and another book was opened, which is the book of life: and the dead were judged out of those things which were written in the books, according to their works. And the sea gave up the dead which were in it; and death and hell delivered up the dead which were in them: and they were judged every man according to their works. And death and hell were cast into the lake of fire. This is the second death."

By His grace, we need not wait until we stand before the Throne of God at the Judgement to confess Christ Jesus as

Lord. We can do it today! We can be free from the bondages that most of rock music is under. Be free today!

Heavenly Father,
Thank you for opening my eyes and heart to see that the music industry has been used by the enemy to destroy many people. By Your grace, Lord, I now have the chance to be free. Please deliver me from the bondage of the culture of rock music so that I will not let bad lyrics run through my ears, into my mind and down to my heart anymore. I now know that garbage into the heart produces garbage going out. I ask you to help me find Christian music that I can enjoy and receive light and love by which I may be able to reflect that light rather than the darkness I have been reflecting to my friends and family from bad music. Thank you Lord for delivering and saving me!

In Jesus' Name,
Amen!

Chapter 4

SATAN'S DEVICES

2 Corinthians 2:11, "….Lest Satan should get an advantage of us: for we are not ignorant of his devices."

Many people today have wondered "Could technology go wrong?" It's a question that Hollywood has entertained with movies like Arthur C Clarks, Science Fiction thriller; "2001 A Space Odyssey", where a computer named Hal, takes over and begins to think as a person. "War Games" was a movie that was fun to watch when I was a teenager. It was about a military super-computer named Joshua which could not tell reality from a game, but was able to learn.

A more frightening question is "Could technology fall into the wrong hands?" The classic book, *1984*, written by Eric Arthur Blair under the pen name, George Orwell, is one of the best examples, not of technology itself being evil, but of the users of technology being evil. Though there is no solid evidence to support the claim, George Orwell was rumored to have worked with British intelligentsia to develop mind control, and this was a major theme in his book, "1984." This book was written in 1948 and now its chilling futuristic predictions are being manifested in our generation. In fact the concept of "Big Brother" we see today even surpasses the "doublethink" envisioned in the book.

"Doublethink" as defined by Webster's Dictionary is "a simultaneous belief in two contradictory ideas." In George Orwell's *1984,* the character Winston Smith, who worked as a clerk in the "Ministry of Truth" office rewriting historical documents, explains "doublethink" like this: "To know and not to know, to be conscious of complete truthfulness while telling carefully constructed lies, to hold simultaneously two opinions which cancelled out, knowing them to be contradictory and believing in both of them, to use logic against logic, to repudiate morality while laying claim to it, to believe that democracy was impossible and that the Party was the guardian of democracy, to forget whatever it was necessary to forget, then to draw it back into memory again at the moment when it was needed, and then promptly to forget it again: and above all, to apply the same process to the process itself. That was the ultimate subtlety: consciously to induce unconsciousness, and then, once again, to become unconscious of the act of hypnosis you had just performed. Even to understand the word 'doublethink' involved the use of 'doublethink'."

Doublethink is really just saying that good is evil, evil is good; something that is happening with more frequency and intensity every day. Society has declined to the point of depicting God as the bad guy. Jesus Christ, Who was the meek and lowly Son of Man, Who submitted Himself to do the Father's will, and died an innocent Man, is openly hated and mocked. As Isaiah prophesied of Christ, **"He is brought as a lamb to the**

slaughter, and as a sheep before her shearers is dumb,
so he openeth not his mouth." Isaiah 53:7(b).** Even many
Christians embrace Gay Churches and cheer the missions of
the U.S. Military Industrial Complex, such as "Shock and Awe,"
which kill many innocents in faraway lands. **Isaiah 5:20** warns,
**"Woe unto them that call evil good, and good evil; that put
darkness for light, and light for darkness; that put bitter
for sweet, and sweet for bitter!"**

"Big Brother", in Orwell's book, was the system of cameras
and microphones that could hear and see everyone and everything everywhere. Currently, this title goes to the U.S. Secretary
of Homeland Security, Janet Napolitano. They call her "Big
Sis".(66) She got this moniker from her "See Something, Say
Something" campaign, which ran at Wal-Mart's nationwide. The
nickname was meant as an insult from those who did not agree
that the "masses" who shop at Wal-Mart could be brainwashed
into tattle telling, and spying on their neighbors. Her tenure is
also responsible, for making the now infamous list of potential
terrorists, which includes:

- Americans who believe their "way of life" is under attack;
- Americans who are "fiercely nationalistic"(as opposed to
  universal and international in orientation);
- People who consider themselves "anti-global" (presumably
  those who are wary of the loss of American sovereignty);
- Americans who are "suspicious of centralized federal
  authority";
- Americans who are "reverent of individual liberty";
- People who "believe in conspiracy theories that involve grave
  threat to national sovereignty and/or personal liberty."(67)

Aldous Huxley was the first to blow away the satanic smoke of deception that a man-made utopian civilization without God was possible. Huxley said that *Brave New World* was inspired by the utopian novels of H.G. Wells, including *A Modern Utopia* (1905) and *Men Like Gods* (1923).(68) Wells' hopeful vision of the future's possibilities gave Huxley the idea to begin writing a parody of the novel, which became *Brave New World*.

The concept of humanity being able to create its own utopia, or paradise, was promoted by men like H.G. Wells prior to WW I. After the "War to End All Wars" ended in 1918, leaving 20 million dead, it was evident that mankind was not progressing towards utopia, as many Illuminists had predicted. Aldous Huxley also exposed the loss of privacy and personal identity in a future planned by the occult minded writers like Wells.

The term "predictive programming" refers to the idea of conditioning the public to buy into a vision of the future that the powers that be (elite) want to enact. It is done by gradually and subtly inculcating the masses with the ideas that the elite want to promulgate so that when the predictions truly begin to come to pass, people are already used to the concepts and accepting of them. H.G. Wells' books, *The Shape of Things to Come* and *The Work, Wealth and Happiness of Mankind*, were part of this "predictive programming" process. They introduced many things about modern warfare: atom bombs, the United Nations, stealth fighters, space travel and countless other details of the future. He also laid plans for the how the New World Order should be created.

Wells was involved in creating the League of Nations. During the Russian Revolution he went to Russia to visit Lenin, and discuss the creation of a New World Order. They ended up not liking each other, and never met again. But later, Wells met with President Roosevelt. Both H.G. Wells, and FDR were Freemasons and their meeting went better than the meeting with Lenin had. Wells said of his meeting with Roosevelt that the "United States...[was] the most effective transmitting instrument possible for the coming of the new world order."(69)

As an aside, it was Franklin D. Roosevelt, under the influence of his Secretary of Agriculture, Henry Wallace, who put the now famous Great Seal of the United States on the back of the dollar bill. The mysterious seal, having been created in 1782, contains the saying *Annuit cœptis Novus ordo seclorum*, which literally translates from the Latin to "favorably beginning new world order." It was the announcement of the New World Order of the Ages. Later Wallace would become the Vice President of the United Stated (1941-1945) during FDR's second term in office. During the presidential campaign, news media sources exposed the fact that during his tenure as Secretary of Agriculture, Wallace had a evil spiritual advisor, an occultist luminary named Nicolas Rohric, who he called "Guru" in his correspondence.(70) Rohric introduced Wallace to "Theosophy", a philosophy and religion promoted by Madam Helena Blavatsky which combines eastern religion and Western esoteric teachings. From two Greek words, *theos*, meaning "divine", and s*ophia* meaning "wisdom", Theosophy teaches ancient mysteries and knowledge can be attained by connecting one's inner deity to nature by way of occult practices.(71)

Daniel 12:4, "But thou, O Daniel, shut up the words, and seal the book, even to the time of the end: many shall run to and fro, and knowledge shall be increased."

Daniel prophesied that in the End Times, knowledge would increase; and it has done so at a staggering pace in recent history. The leading indicator of this global increase of knowledge and information is technology. So quickly is technology advancing that the cell phone, computer, software, i-pads, mp3s (any gadget currently available), will likely be obsolete within six months to two years.

Imagine Julius Caesar (born 100 BC) being able to travel forward in time, about 1800 years, to the time of George Washington and the founding of the USA in the late 1700's. Think about these two Generals riding together on the battlefield. Would Caesar be totally lost? Would he be amazed at the progress and changes that had taken place in those 1,800 years? Well, the funny thing is, No. Most things were still the same. There was no electricity, only whale oil or similar fuel for lamps. Battles were still fought on horseback with swords. Gun powder would have been one of the only new inventions. It was not until the U.S. Civil war that doctors began to realize that washing hands between patients reduced infections.

Now, imagine this: General Washington travels forward in time to 2013, on the battlefield in Afghanistan. This quantum leap is only 250 years. (It was 1,800 years from the time of Julius Caesar to the American Revolutionary War.) So, would General Washington be lost? Or would he be able to adapt quickly to the modern battlefield? In all likelihood he would be totally overwhelmed by contemporary military technology: radios, computers, Global Positioning Satellite, tanks, missiles, airplanes, bombs. Atomic bombs, guided missiles, video feeds, real-time feed back to the front lines (and to the President of the United States ½ way around the globe!), modern medicine, cell phones (any phone!), Night vision goggles, infrared goggles, drones. These are only a few implements of the present-day battlefield. His whole way of life and thinking would be turned completely upside-down. A Civil War General would be no less amazed at modern warfare than his Revolutionary War counterpart. Just think that in less than 150 years, we have moved from no cars, no planes, no electricity (in fact even Kerosene lamps were not invented until 1868, three years after the end of the U.S. Civil War) to the information age!

Remember the old days of writing a letter or postcard? Remember having to stay home and wait for a phone call for a job interview or a date? Remember when someone wanted to know a trivial fact about something they called the local librarian? Those were the good old days, before Google, and cell phones, before the term "snail mail" was invented. People were use to waiting. Americans bragged about how in the Old West, it took months to get a letter by way of Pony Express. Then the train was invented. People thought, "Wow, it can't get any better than this!" Now we can reach out and find our old Army buddies on Facebook or other internet social media in minutes. It all is so fun and great to see!

But wait! What if the IRS decides they want to know if you are being honest? They can look up your Facebook page, check your status, and see the posts of your vacation to Rome which you had claimed as a "business trip" on your taxes. Now it's audit time!

Remember Harriton High School near Philadelphia, Pennsylvania, that put a program on the free MacBook laptops they gave to all students, so they could spy on them via the computers' built-in webcam? The community found out, when the school called in students to discipline them for things they did at home, in front of the camera. It apparently had not even occurred to the school that what it was doing might be illegal. The school officials were shocked that parents got upset! It took a February 2010 Federal Judge's order that the district stop activating the cameras on the school issued laptops to finally end the spying.(72) This is the Orwellian world we find ourselves in today.

Satan has a plan for technology and he will implement it during the last seven years of world history before the Second Coming of Christ. Knowledge has increased now to the level needed to fulfill biblical prophecy. This is, in itself a sign of the End of the Age as Daniel 12:4(b) says "knowledge shall be increased."

Revelation 11 speaks of two witnesses killed by the Beast whose bodies will be seen around the world. **"And their dead bodies shall lie in the street of the great city, which spiritually is called Sodom and Egypt, where also our Lord was crucified.[9] And <u>they of the people and kindreds and tongues and nations shall see their dead bodies three days and an half</u>, and shall not suffer their dead bodies to be put in graves.[10] And they that dwell upon the earth shall rejoice over them, and make merry, and shall send gifts one to another; because these two prophets tormented them that dwelt on the earth.[11] And after three days and an half the spirit of life from God entered into them, and they stood upon their feet; and great fear fell upon them which saw them." Revelation 11:8-11.**

This event, predicted over 1900 years ago, has only been possible since the advent of satellite television in 1963.

Furthermore, most people around the world have not had a TV or a cable or satellite connection until last several years.

In 2007 the "Connect Africa Initiative", spearheaded by technology companies around the world, began working to establish data infrastructure on the African Continent. The United Nations declared internet access to be a "human right" on June 3, 2011, when it issued this statement: "Given that the Internet has become an indispensable tool for realizing a range of human rights, combating inequality, and accelerating development and human progress, ensuring universal access to the Internet should be a priority for all states." Shortly after this declaration, "Connect the Caribbean Initiative", "Connect Asia-Pacific Summit", and "Connect Arab Summit 2012" were simultaneously begun. These three global connection programs are on track to be completed in 2015.(73) Another unique trend in technology is that many Christian television channels have moved and are moving to Jerusalem. This is also setting the stage for Revelation 11 to come to pass. I believe these stations will be instrumental in reaching the Jewish people who will accept Jesus Christ as their Messiah after the Rapture. From these stations, broadcasts of the events as they unfold in Israel—which will be the eye of the coming world-wide storm—will be seen around the world.

As this chapter is being written, the news has exploded with reports of Government spying:

ABCNews, May 7, 2013, "US Governement Monitoring Phone Calls, Emails and Internet Activity"

UK Daily Mail, May 12, 2013, "Interactive TV Spies on Viewers"

Reuters, June 7, 2013, "NSA Spying Included Major Internet Companies"

Info Security, June 11, 2013," Operation PRISM: NSA and FBI monitoring activity at Facebook, Apple, Google, and other tech firms"

Gateway Press, June 12, 2013, "IRS seen Training with AR15s"

Chicago Tribune, June 20, 2013, "FBI uses drones inside U.S. for spying, director says"

BBC News June 26, 2013, "US whistleblower [Gov. cell phone spying scandal] Snowden 'still in Moscow airport' "

The Federal Government is spying on us and now they are so bold as to admit it! This is all in preparation if the Kingdom of the Anti-Christ and the Mark of the Beast system. Things are happen faster than I can write them down! This chapter, which I began writing as events that would unfold in the near future, is now coming true even before this book has gone to print! So let's not waste anymore time covering the history of technology, let's just summarize by saying this: Technology has exploded, just as the Bible said it would, in the last days, with knowledge doubling every six months or LESS. Daniel 12:4 has been, and continues to be fulfilled right before our very eyes!

Robert Mueller, Director of the United States Federal Bureau of Investigation has admitted to using their spy drones to monitor US Citizens. The Federal Government has also acknowledged their data mining and storage of all emails, phone calls and other electronic communication. The next public announcement may well be that experiments are underway (or have already been done) to develop "super-humans" . Transhumanism, the restructuring of human DNA using technology, is the next horizon of the "Brave New World" that is dawning. It will be cloaked as something good, such as altering DNA to eradicate debilitating diseases. But everything good is twisted by Satan.

Could it be that the Mark of the Beast, the infamous 666, will involve some Transhumanist result? People who take it will have promises of near immortality and perfect health, perhaps even superhuman power. Could it be that the DNA of a cat could be used for night vision, the DNA of an ape for strength? Will a chip be devised to impart knowledge? A chip to become a doctor, instantly, no more spending six to eight years in medical school and another six to eight years as a resident. Just take the chip! As I am writing this today, the UK Daily Mail headline is "We'll be uploading our entire MINDS to computers by 2045 and our bodies will be replaced by machines within 90 years, Google expert claims."(74)

Things are changing so fast, it is futile to try to follow it all. (Author and retired pastor of 25 years, Dr Tom Horn, has written many books on the subject of Transhumanism. I recommend them to those who desire to know the exhaustive details of these matters.) I will not attempt to zoom in on the limitless details, but rather suffice to ask this question: Since we are clearly on the brink of the New World Order and the Kingdom of the Anti-Christ, what are we going to do about it?

All of this technology can be, is being, and will be turned against us, to control us, and to Mark those who are left behind after the Rapture. Earth will be the "prison planet" during the

Tribulation. The Antichrist will announce that all must swear allegiance to him, like the Caesars of the Roman Empire did during the time of the early Church. Anyone who refuses will be beheaded.

Revelation 20:4: "And I saw thrones, and they sat upon them, and judgment was given unto them: and <u>I saw the souls of them that were beheaded</u> for the witness of Jesus, and for the word of God, and which had not worshipped the beast, neither his image, neither had received his mark upon their foreheads, or in their hands; and they lived and reigned with Christ a thousand years."

Anyone who does NOT take the Mark, will not be able to work, or buy food. How will those left behind survive? Can survivalist escape the drones and satellites overhead? Or the zombie-like people who will take the Mark and be under the control of the Anti-Christ who will surely be rewarded for turning in anyone without the Mark of the Beast to the authorities. **Revelation 13:17, "And that <u>no man might buy or sell</u>, save he that had the mark, or the name of the beast, or the number of his name."**

That day is fast approaching, time is almost up. Our Lord Jesus Christ said, **"when you see all these signs"** (Like those presented *throughout this book!*) **"know that it is near EVEN AT THE DOOR!"** (Matthew 24:33, Mark 13:9) As the story of Cain in the Bible, God told him, sin is lying at your door. (**Genesis 4:7, "If thou doest well, shalt thou not be accepted? and if thou doest not well, sin lieth at the door."**) You must not let sin get you!

So, what are YOU going to do about it? Are you Born-Again? Have you experienced the life-changing, heart-transforming effects of an authentic encounter with our Lord Jesus Christ, or are you "Christian" in name only? As the old hymn asks, "Are you fully trusting in His grace this hour? Are you washed in the Blood of the lamb?" If you cannot answer an unequivocal "yes" to these questions, you need to immediately call upon the name of the Lord! Right now. Do not waste another second being "double minded", as the Bible calls it. There is no time to sit on the fence and play with the world. Today is your day to know that you are on your way to Heaven, that you are saved and at peace with God. For the Bible tells us, **in Romans 8:16, "The Spirit itself beareth witness with our spirit, that we are the children of God."** With all these things in mind, it is time for you to present yourself before the Lord God Almighty, and stay there until your spirit, KNOWS that you have been sealed by His Spirit.

Dear Heavenly Father,
I know that I am a sinner. I know I have done so many bad things. Right now I think of those things I wish never happened, and I think if I could just go back so that they would never have happened, I could have a new start and overcome my mistakes. Lord, I ask you to forgive me. Please cleanse me from my past. You are the Lord of the Harvest. Cancel the bad harvest from the bad seed I have sowed. Please give me a new harvest, a new start, so that I may serve You, and bring glory to Your Name. Save me, Lord, from what I deserve. I know that You died for me. I receive Your forgiveness and love. I believe You are the Resurrection and the Life. Though I was dead until now, I will

live, starting today! By your grace, I am made whole! Thank You, Father, in Jesus' Name, Amen!

If you prayed that prayer from your heart, you are on your way to heaven, just as much as a person who has been a Christian for 40 years! Praise the Lord for His mercy on us all! Please email me and tell me about it! I want to rejoice with you and pray for you! You can find my email in the "About the Author" section of this book.

Chapter 5

SATAN'S SEDUCTIONS

1 Timothy 4:1-2: "Now the Spirit speaketh expressly, that in the latter times some shall depart from the faith, giving heed to seducing spirits, and doctrines of devils; Speaking lies in hypocrisy; having their conscience seared with a hot iron"

Picture American circa 1950's: Baseball, hotdogs, apple pie, and good old fashion life, before TV, before prayer was taken out of school, and before Rock n roll. In 1950 "gay" was a synonym for happy, a "partner" was a business associate, and "getting high" meant climbing a mountain. We threw rocks and rolled balls. Sex education was left to the parents. The illegitimate birth rate in 1950 was extremely low and crime rates were ½ that of today.(75) Drug use was virtually non-existent and the schools complained of problems such as chewing gum and talking in line. Life was very much like *The Andy Griffith Show* for most of America.

Here are some statistics from the decade of the 1950's:

*the GDP grew by 250%

*average incomes tripled

*the housing market was booming

*1.5 million homes per year were being built

*Home ownership rates exploded

*60% of Americans were "middle class"

*Poverty rates were dropping rapidly

*Consumer spending doubled in the 1950s

*Divorce rates were low, marriage rates were high and people
   married at a younger age than at any other time in history

*Only 4% of children were born out-of-wedlock, compared
   to 40% today

*90% of children grew up with married parents

*there was no crack epidemic

*discipline problems in school were minor

*the US educational system was the world's finest at the time

*cost of living was low

*families lived comfortably on only one income

*Americans believed home & family were society's most
   important element

*No secular humanist movement opposed the 1954 addition
   of "under God" to the Pledge of Allegiance.

*The birth rate was high, women had almost 4 children on
   average (76)

Even though women had fewer job opportunities and there
was more racial tension in the 1950's, the family unit was strong
and thriving. In fact the 1950s may have been nearly as idyllic

as "Leave it to Beaver," the classic television series, seemed to suggest. In the 1950's, minimum wage workers could pay their monthly rent for less than a week and a half of full-time work. Federal income tax rates were higher, 17.4% for median income earners vs. 15% today, but the lower cost of living made it easier for families to do well. Back then minimum wage was $0.75 per hour; the average price per gallon of gas was $0.27, which represented wages for 22 minutes of work; average movie ticket price was $0.48 (wages for 38 minutes of work); and the median rent was $42 per month (wages for 56 hours). (77) The average wage earner made $2,686 which is equivalent to $24,406 in today's dollars and was far closer to the $2500 per year that the minimum wage earner's annual earnings than today's figures of $14,500 per year for minimum wage vs. the $42,979 average wages of 2011.(78) So if people were able to live better on less income in the 1950's, what has changed? The short answer is that most families today are two income households. When more money is flowing into the economy, inflation is the result. But this is a known economic principle, so what would entice a population to such a thing?

Dr. Henry Makow, writer of the Canadian syndicated advice to parents column, "Ask Henry", has said "There is no more fundamental yet delicate relationship in society than male and female. The family, the red blood cell of society, depends upon it. Nobody with the interests of society at heart would try to divide men and women. Yet the lie that men have exploited women has become the official orthodoxy."(79) The feminist movement is the spring from which flows many tributaries to the decline of American society: The "Right to Privacy" and the legalization of birth control, abortion rights, women leaving the home for the workplace, the sexual revolution, the breakdown of the family, even the homosexual (or LGBT) agenda has its ultimate origins in feminism.

The sexual revolution was one of the things Aleister Crowley (see Satan's Sages) wrote about in his books. Although the changes started out small, as gradual adjustments in the way society perceives sexuality, they have now snowballed into an avalanche of change that is increasing in speed and magnitude every day. As of this writing, 13 of the United States and many countries worldwide have legalized "Gay marriage." This was one of Crowley's satanically-channeled concepts, to see sodomy as celebrated and to use it to destroy the Church by destroying the family.

BIRTH CONTROL:

Margaret Sanger (1879-1966) preached the gospel of a woman's "right to choose" motherhood; it was termed "voluntary motherhood." Her assumptions that the societal norms of "first comes love, then come marriage, then comes the baby carriage" were outdated and oppressive to women. To be sure, some marriages were abusive and some women were held hostage by their economic circumstances, unfortunately those cases still occur today. But, Sanger's promotion of birth control as necessary to an individual woman's physical and mental health and freedom was not initially well received among the majority. She was accused of promoting "free love" and even jailed in 1915 publishing information on contraceptives. The prosecutor used the 1873 Comstock Act which banned the sale and dissemination of pornographic material. Margaret Sanger continued her fight for birth control availability by having a shipment of Japanese made diaphragms sent to a sympathetic New York physician. As expected, the package was detained by customs in New York harbor. Sanger funded the lawyer for the physician, and the result was the 1936 Federal Appeals Court ruling, *United States v One Package of Japanese Pessaries,* that the Federal Government could not interfere with a physicians right to provide contraceptive devices to patients.(80)

The Birth Control Movement of the 1930's was actually aimed at limiting the procreation of the "colored" race. Its founder, Margaret Sanger, was racist even by 1930's standards. Her first clinic in Harlem was opened in 1930 and staffed with doctors from the black community. The founder of the NAACP, W.E.B. Dubois, promoted the clinic in black churches with funding from the Urban League. In the 1940's, Sanger's Birth Control Federation of America (BCFA) initiated the "Negro Project," with the stated purpose being to improve prenatal care and infant health, but with the secondary (some would argue, primary) goal of reducing pregnancies among poor black women using the only birth control method of the time, condoms.(81) .

The use of condoms became widespread and was promoted by the U.S. Military during WW I because of their effectiveness in preventing diseases such as syphilis and gonorrhea. But during the 1930's and early 1940's condoms were most widely available through Margaret Sanger's BCFA. Advocating and facilitating the use of birth control among one select segment of the population is eugenics, racism, pure and simple.

When diseases become involved, sex is no longer a moral issue but a public health concern. The Military's anti-venereal disease campaign of the 1940's was instrumental in moving the topic of sexuality from the privacy of the family unit to the open forum of communicable disease prevention. But, in the 1940's the "purity movement" was very strong, so the official government stance on the topic was to remain abstinent in order to prevent pregnancy and disease.

Then came the 1960's.

Margaret Sanger, the founder of BCFA, and later, Planned Parenthood, had the idea of a pill to prevent pregnancy and used her influence to persuade physicians and scientists to begin the process of developing pharmaceutical contraceptives. In 1951, Sanger secured funding for birth control pill research. She continued to raise funds and provide critical support so that by 1954, the birth control pill was being tested in humans. The first birth control pill was approved by the U.S. Food and Drug Administration (FDA) in 1957 for the treatment of menstrual problems. Then in 1960, the pill was approved for sale as a contraceptive.[82] We are not here to discuss the morality of the birth control pill. Everyone accepts the fact that couples have to plan their families. Even though some within the Christian community hold the conviction that any form of artificial birth control is wrong, this is a personal matter of conscience and belief, and our purpose is not to argue for or against this issue, but to show that just as God can use what was meant as evil for good (Genesis 50:20), Satan can use what was meant as good for evil.

The 1965 *Griswald vs. Connecticut* Supreme Court case was a landmark decision in that it established the "right to privacy" by a vote of 7 to 2. The *Griswald* case overturned Connecticut's 1879 law against the use of "any drug, medicinal article or instrument for the purpose of preventing contraception," saying that a couple had the "right to marital privacy."[83] While this decision certainly seems reasonable today, Satan can use even reasonable and well-intentioned actions for evil.

The earliest birth control pills prevented ovulation with high doses of estrogen, but came with very unpleasant side effects. Because they induced a state of "pseudo-pregnancy," those who took the pill could have nausea, weight gain, blurred vision, depression, blood clots even stroke—any complication of pregnancy could be a side effect. So the search for an improved pill began and modern low dose birth control pills were the result.

Low dose birth control pills prevent pregnancy in 3 ways: (1) inhibition of ovulation, (2) inhibition of sperm transport, and (3) production of a 'hostile endometrium', which prevents or disrupts implantation of the developing baby if the first two mechanisms fail. A "disruption" of implantation of a fertilized egg is, of course, a miscarriage. The *Physician's Desk Reference* (PDR) in describing the effects of all name-brand birth control pills, states that the BCP has "progestational effect on the endometrium, interfering with implantation." And, "... alterations in ...the endometrium which reduce the likelihood of implantation."(84)

In the New York Times of Thursday, April 27, 1989, transcript of the oral arguments in the Supreme Court case of *Webster v. Reproductive Health Services*, pB13, records the following dialogue between Frank Susman, lawyer for the Missouri abortion clinics and Justice Scalia:

Mr. Susman: "For better or worse, there no longer exists any bright line between the fundamental right that was established in *Griswold* and the fundamental right of abortion that was established in *Roe*. These two rights, because of advances in medicine and science, now overlap. They coalesce and merge and they are not distinct."

Justice Scalia: "Excuse me, you find it hard to draw a line between those two but easy to draw a line between (the) first, second and third trimester."

Mr. Susman: "I do not find it difficult."

Justice Scalia: "I don't see why a court that can draw that line can't separate abortion from birth control quite readily."

Mr. Susman: "If I may suggest the reasons in response to your question, Justice Scalia. The most common forms of what we most generally in common parlance call contraception today, IUD's, low-dose birth control pills, which are the safest type of birth control pills available, act as abortifacients. They are correctly labeled as both.
Under this statute, which defines fertilization as the point of beginning, those forms of contraception are also abortifacients. Science and medicine refer(s) to them as both. We are not still dealing with the common barrier methods of *Griswold*. We are no longer just talking about condoms and diaphragms.
Things have changed. The bright line, if there ever was one, has now been extinguished. That's why I suggest to this Court that we need to deal with one right, the right to procreate. We are no longer talking about two rights."

Mr. Susman is arguing that, if birth control pills are legal, then abortion ought to be as well. This conversation illustrates just how Satan operates! He uses even what at first seems good and twists it into something sinister. And the pawns in his game plan do not even realize they are being played. The result of the birth control pill was sex without consequences which led to Free Love which led to abortion and pornography. The pill allowed women to pursue careers, which in turn began to change society's attitude toward motherhood.

The concept of Free Love expressed by hippies of the 1960's meant freedom "to love whomever you pleased, whenever you pleased, however you pleased."(85) Spontaneous sexual activity and experimentation was encouraged and celebrated. The Hippies of the 1960's engaged in group sex, public sex, sex with minors, homosexuality—any and all taboos went out the window. Monogamous heterosexual sex between married couples, though still the norm, was no longer the only acceptable environment for sexual expression among the open relationships of the 1960's. Among the hippy culture of Free Love, if a partner in a relationship was attracted to another, s/he could explore that relationship without animosity or jealousy. In other words, it was a lifestyle of consensual serial fornication. Their mantra: "If it feels good, do it!"

The hippie movement reached its peak in the late 1960's, during the height of the Vietnam Conflict. It is estimated that around 100,000 people traveled to San Francisco for the 1967 "Summer of Love" event. The news media covered the event and cast the spotlight on their "make love not war" ideal. Wide media coverage of the movement continued into the 1969 Woodstock Festival, attended by 300,000 young people. But by mid-1970's the media of the hippie movement had also exposed their pro-drug and anti-work penchants, which during the heightened national pride of the American Bicentennial in 1976, contributed to that movement's decline. The ideals of "free love" however, were not completely abandoned.

ABORTION:

Then in 1973 the Supreme Court legalized abortion. Relying heavily on the "right to privacy" established in the 1965 *Griswald* case, the court said that a woman had the right to terminate her pregnancy until the fetus was viable. Despite that decision, the Bible remains pro-life. Psalm 129:13-14, NRSV, says **"For it was You who formed my inward parts; You knit me together in my mother's womb. I praise You, for I am fearfully *and* wonderfully made; Marvelous are Your works, *that* I know very well."**

Mother Teresa said at the 1994 National Prayer Breakfast, "… [Abortion] is really a war against the child, and I hate the killing of the innocent child, murder by the mother herself. And if we accept that the mother can kill even her own child, how can we tell other people not to kill one another?… By abortion, the mother does not learn how to live, but kills even her own child to solve her problem. And by abortion, the father is taught that he does not have to take any responsibility at all for the child he has brought into the world. So that father is likely to put other women into the same trouble. So abortion just leads to more abortion. Any country that accepts abortion is not teaching its people to love one another but to use any violence to get what they want. This is why the greatest destroyer of love and peace is abortion."

Abortion is also a celebration of death, and an offering unto Satan. As the Bible tells us, in the last days, humanity would be "without natural affection." (Romans 1:31, 2 Timothy 3:3)

114

What could be more "without natural affection" than to kill one's own baby? How blind and sick has this world become that any human, could be so heartless and ignorant as to justify in their own mind, the killing of their own flesh and blood!

This alone should be proof positive that the devil is VERY real, and more than capable of blinding the hearts of the lost. All of the sexual revolution was planned by Satan, to kill, steal and destroy the family.

Let me just add an ironic note at this point, because many Christians are on the other end of this comparison I will make: There are many "liberal" non-Christian types, who will decry the loss of life in a war such as that in Iraq and Afghanistan during the so called, "war on terror". Yet, they support abortion as a "woman's right" to "reproductive health." However on the opposite end of the spectrum, many so-called "conservative" Christians, will cheer at the military might used to secure oil fields for the elite, (who will bring the antichrist to power with their ill gotten gains) and fully support the military industrial complex's money making war machine that has killed hundreds of thousands of innocent civilians, many of them children. As you may have realized, Iraq, was in no way connected to 9-11. Yet, these "Christians" are against abortions but pro-war.

As a Gulf War veteran, I have seen firsthand many things that prove undeniably, that many of our troops not only love to kill, but that they see the local people as subhuman. This is very much like the Nazis' attitude toward the Jews. I have witnessed soldiers who play death metal music to get fired up or "psyched up," to kill with pleasure.

Violence has now pervaded our culture, with just as many policemen becoming cold and wicked, as there are soldiers who love to kill. This is evident on the evening news and in the morning paper's accounts of more and more police violence. There was a time when law enforcement officers were gentlemen and women were only very rarely criminals. Now, after almost a half century of telling women they can behave just like men, they are doing so.

Since *Roe v Wade,* over 55,000,000 children have been killed in their mother's wombs and violence against children has escalated on all sides. For example, school shootings have increased dramatically, with the second half of the decade of the 1970's being one of the most violent periods in U.S. School history. There were 13 school shootings from 1973 to 1979, resulting in the death of 21 people. And the violence has only increased. The December 14, 2012, Sandy Hook Elementary School shootings claimed the lives of 20 children and 6 adults. Mother Teresa's logic seems to have been correct, "If we accept that the mother can kill even her own child, how can we tell other people not to kill each other?" Couple this with the Supreme Court Case, *Abingdon School District v. Schempp,* which ten years prior, in 1963, had removed prayer from schools, then add the1968 Supreme Court decision, *Epperson v. Arkansas*, which ruled that Arkansas' State law against the teaching of evolution in its public schools violated the First Amendment, (Freedom of Speech). The result: Generations of children brought up without traditional, Biblical, values and standards of behavior that come from knowing that we are created in the image and likeness of God. (Genesis 1:27)

Abortion is so commonplace now that 1 in every 2 1/2 women (about 40%) in the USA will have had an abortion by the time they are 45 years old. Abortion is a permanent solution to a temporary problem. Once the temporary problem is solved, even if the women felt perfectly justified in her decision at the time of her abortion, she will eventually realize the gravity of that permanent solution. Women who have had abortions are prone to depression and guilt at one end—PTSD (Post Traumatic Stress Disorder) symptoms at the other end. Who can imagine any woman being *un*affected by her abortion?

The medical community has shied away from studying the issue, so groups like Rachel Vineyard, Ramah International and others have done research, which of course the left dismisses for bias.(86) But God has not dismissed these women or their pain. Jesus was not exaggerating or using metaphor when He said, **"Ask and it will be given to you; seek and you will find; knock and the door will be opened to you"** (Matthew 7:7). He will apply His grace to everyone who searches for it.

God's free gift of forgiveness is beyond our comprehension; but when we cooperate with His desire for wholeness and healing by asking for that forgiveness He gives liberally, even lavishly. Recall the story of the Prodigal Son. The Father saw him coming a great way off and ran to meet him. As the hymn, *The Love of God* proclaims, "His erring child, he reconciles and pardons from his sin." He will run to meet any sinner who repents. Isaiah prophesied 700 years before the time of Christ: **"But He was pierced for our transgressions, He was crushed for our iniquities; the punishment that brought us PEACE was upon Him, and by His wounds we are healed"** (Isaiah 53:5 NIV).

Peace is found in Jesus.

CHANGING ATTITUDES:

Turning away from the knowledge of the One True God has produced no good thing for society. Since Prayer was taken out of schools 50 years ago, premarital sex among teens is up 500%, unwed pregnancies up 400%, STDs have increased by 200%, suicide has risen 400%, violent crime rate is 500% higher and SAT scores have dropped 90 points. In 1963, America's education system was the envy of the world. Now, the USA ranks last in SAT scores in the industrialized world.

In 1950, less than 12% of women with children worked outside the home; but by 2010, that figure was close to 70%.(87) Society's message to families is one of consumerism: bigger, better, more. Two income families not only need a house and a car, but a bigger house and two cars. Women are conditioned to believe that they need to work to be equal to a man, that they CAN have it all, bringing home the bacon, and frying it up in the pan like the fantasy feminist ideal of 1979 Enjoli perfume commercial. Women have been enticed into believing the exaggeration of extremes of the woman in the ad who splits into three roles: the go-getting woman working outside of the home; the bathrobe clad lady with a frying pan tending to hearth and home; and the sensual, seductive woman in the pink night gown who is, after her busy day, still energetic enough for an evening of romance. Men are told that they are sexist if they do not support their wives. But those who are most harmed by this reinterpretation of Biblical family roles are the children.

Perhaps it is merely coincidental that from the decade of the 1950's through 1967, the divorce rate in America hovered around 25%. But all of that began to change in 1970 when "no fault" divorce laws began to be passed in many states. Touted by feminist as a means to make it easier for women to escape an abusive marriage, the divorce rate has rapidly spiked since these laws have taken effect. These are the divorce rates from 1970 to 1985 according to a 2011 U.S. Census Bureau report: 1970, 33%, 1975, 48%; 1980, 52%; 1985, 50%. (88)

Even though divorce rates have leveled off, and even begun to drop slightly since 1985, a new trend is now in play, namely that many people are choosing not to ever marry at all. The result is that, according to a March 2013 report by the National Marriage Project (NMP), 48% of all first born babies are born outside of wedlock. People are deciding to marry only after they have they have finished their education, started a career, and have gotten their finances in order. This may work out fine for the college educated (only 37% of their first births are outside wedlock), but not nearly as well for high school dropouts (83% of first births outside of wedlock). The cost for children of unwed parents is often an unstable home life. According to the NMP report, 39% of unmarried parents who begin living together will break up before their child is 5 years old. Only 13% of married parents split when their children are so young.(89)

The unfortunate reality of working mothers and single parenting is that one person cannot do it all. God designed *families* to raise children and He has specific roles for men and women. There is nothing wrong with a woman working and her husband being primarily responsible for the children, especially when the woman has a professional career that brings in more income than her spouse. And obviously in single parent families, mother or father must work. But *someone* needs to be primarily responsible for children, and for many families *neither* parent has time for them. So children are left alone to be latch key kids, coming home after school to an empty house, and receiving their primary instruction from media sources that are at best secular, at worst completely hostile to Christianity: television, internet, radio.

According to a study presented at the American Heart Association's 48th Annual Conference on Cardiovascular Disease Epidemiology and Prevention reported in March 2008's *Science News Daily*, "Most teenagers (60 percent) spend on average 20 hours per week in front of television and computer screens, a third spend closer to 40 hours per week, and about 7 percent are exposed to more than 50 hours of 'screen-time' per week,."(90)

What are kids seeing? Cartoon Network, Comedy Central, Disney Channel, E! Entertainment Television, MTV, MTV2, NICK/Nick at Nite, VHI just to name a small sample of the most popular channels for youngster out of America's Top 250 Cable TV choices.

In 1981, Music Television, or MTV, was launched. It was a new and innovative venue for promoting popular music that seems a match "made in Heaven" (or Hell). It was soon followed by "VH1" (Video Hits 1) and "CMT" (Country Music Television), both of which were huge industry successes. If there had ever been any ambiguity in the minds of music lovers as to the meaning of the lyrics, there would be no doubt now. MTV videos act out in graphic detail just what the artist had in mind when he penned the words to the songs heard on the radio. Sometimes songs, that on the surface seem innocent enough, are revealed in their videos to have deeper perverse, satanic, but always sexual, connotations. Videos such as Christina Aguilera's sexy, seductive offerings can be viewed back-to-back, 24 hours per day, 7 days per week via cable TV and internet. In her video for "Dirty," Aguilera, wearing chaps and a bikini, exclaims to her backup dancers to get "just a little naughty." And they respond with sex simulating dance moves which are little more than pornography set to music.

Sex is being used in advertising as well, to sell everything from hamburgers to underwear to perfume. Victoria's Secret bra and panty commercials seen during prime time viewing hours portray women in a manner that would have been only visible within the pages of Playboy Magazine in the 1970's (And, said magazine would have been wrapped in brown paper and located behind the cash register with the cigarettes, smokeless tobacco and lottery tickets.) Carl Jr.'s Spicy Burger 2005 television commercial features Paris Hilton in a black bathing suit supposedly washing a sports car, although she spent more time rubbing the soapy sponge on herself than on any part of the car, the burger finally appears at the end of the clip when the soaking wet Hilton climbs onto the hood of the vehicle to take a bite. Presumably the car washing has made her hungry. Axe cologne for men rolled out its "Axe Bullet Lets You See through Clothing" ad campaign in 2008 to promote a pocketsize cologne spray. It showed a young man who when wearing Axe had "x-ray" vision, able to see ladies walking their dogs, boarding busses and shopping for groceries in only their bras and panties. Miller Light has even added a new twist to "Taste Great, Less Filling" by having two women in a posh outdoor cafe arguing over why to drink Miller Light. A brawl ensues when one pushes the other into a fountain, they strip down to their underwear, fight their way into a trough of concrete mix, and resolve their differences with a sloppy passionate lesbian kiss on the lips.

The days of chivalry in which women were treated like ladies, protected and honored, have all but vanished in the modern culture. MTV and sex-to-sell by advertising companies are just a few examples of how women have been objectified. Marriage is not even implied in any of these examples. They are all about "free love", sex outside the boundaries God intended. Sex was created by God as "good." It was to be the unifying covenant bond between husband and wife. **Hebrews 13:4, "Marriage is honourable in all, and the bed undefiled: but whoremongers and adulterers God will judge."** This verse tells us that marriage is respectable in every way; and, in particular, sex within marriage is pure, not sullied or debased. But all that God created for good, Satan has desecrated twisted and perverted. (This verse also warns that God will indeed punish fornicators and adulterers.)

HOMOSEXUAL AGENDA:

Not only was abortion legalized and divorce rates on a steep upward climb in 1973, but it was also a pivotal year for homosexuality. 1973 was the year of the history decision by the American Psychiatric Association to declassify homosexuality as a mental disorder. Prior to that decision, psychologists assumed what Sigmund Freud, the father of psychoanalysis, had taught was indeed the case; namely that homosexuality was a symptom of an immature psyche and that it was possible for homosexuals to, with treatment and sufficient motivation, become heterosexual.(91)

The declassification of homosexuality was the first step towards, not only tolerance, but glorification of gay, lesbian, transgender, and bisexual behaviors. Prior to 1970, every State in the Union had anti-sodomy laws on the books. Beginning in 1971, States steadily began legislative repeals of these laws, with the most liberal States repealing them first (Illinois and Connecticut). By 2003, the Supreme Court decision of *Lawrence v. Texas,* invalidated sodomy laws in the remaining 14 States which had not yet repealed them (Alabama, Florida, Idaho, Kansas, Louisiana, Michigan, Missouri, Mississippi, North Carolina, Oklahoma, South Carolina, Texas, Utah, and Virginia) . By 2012, the APA (American Psychiatric Association) adjusted their "Manual of Mental Disorders" (DSM-IV) to include "gender identity disorder," so that people who cannot seem to decide what their gender is can continue to receive treatment paid for by insurance companies (which must have a "diagnosis" to code in order to process payments). In other words, being totally confused about if you are a man or a woman is normal, but the APA is keeping "gender identity disorder" on the books so that multiple sex change operations can be covered by insurance, including Medicaid.(92)

Now, headlines such as these are a regular occurrence:

"Elementary School Hosts Cross-Dressing Day For 1st and 2nd Graders"(93)

"The Evangelical Lutheran Church of America has elected its first openly gay bishop."(94)

"Children's Network Launches Trans-sexual Superhero, SheZow"(95)

"HHS Website for Girls Ages 10 to 16 Informs Youth about Birth Control, Gay Sex, Mutual Masturbation"(96)

"Tumblr post: Gay Teens Voted High School's Cutest Couple Shared 100,000 Times in Just 24 Hours"(97)

"29 Year Old Teacher, Kelly Ann Garcia, Arrested for Having Sex with 16 year old Female Student."(98)

"Transsexuals Challenge "Male/Female" as Outdated Gender IDs"(99)

One bizarre possibility of the tribulation period, which most avoid teaching on, because of the strangeness of it, is the role of the Nephalim. Jesus told us that the time of His Second Coming would be "as it was in the days of Lot" (Luke 17:28) and as the days of Noah Matthew 24. Peter also preached about the End Times, comparing it to the days of Noah and of Lot.

In Genesis 6, we read how the fallen angels slept with human woman, and had giant children. Crazy? Yes! Yet this was the underlining reason for the flood. All flesh had become corrupted. The promised Messiah from Genesis 3:15, the seed of the woman, would not be able to come through the woman if all peoples had their DNA contaminated by the offspring of the Fallen Angels. Jesus said in Matthew 22:30 that angels in Heaven do not get married. That is true, of course. But the fallen angels left their "first estate." "First estate" refers to their place in heaven as well as their heavenly body. They took the form of men. The Holy angels who visited Sodom also temporarily took the form of men. Let's read the text so we can get a clearer understanding.

2 Peter 1:4-9, "For if God spared not the angels that sinned, but cast them down to hell, and delivered them into chains of darkness, to be reserved unto judgment;⁵ And spared not the old world, but saved Noah the eighth person, a preacher of righteousness, bringing in the flood upon the

world of the ungodly;[6] And turning the cities of Sodom and Gomorrha into ashes condemned them with an overthrow, making them an ensample unto those that after should live ungodly;[7] And delivered just Lot, vexed with the filthy conversation of the wicked:[8] (For that righteous man dwelling among them, in seeing and hearing, vexed his righteous soul from day to day with their unlawful deeds;)[9] The Lord knoweth how to deliver the godly out of temptations, and to reserve the unjust unto the day of judgment to be punished"

Yet the book of Jude gives some of the most fascinating insight into the "days of Lot."

Jude 1:5-7, " I will therefore put you in remembrance, though ye once knew this, how that the Lord, having saved the people out of the land of Egypt, afterward destroyed them that believed not. And the angels which kept not their first estate, but left their own habitation, he hath reserved in everlasting chains under darkness unto the judgment of the great day. Even as Sodom and Gomorrah, and the cities about them in like manner, giving themselves over to fornication, and going after strange flesh, are set forth for an example, suffering the vengeance of eternal fire."

Notice that verse 7 begins, "Even as." This is a comparative conjunction linking the example of the "angels which kept not their first estate" and "Sodom and Gomorrah." What is the link between these two? Jude tells us that it is "giving themselves over to fornication, and going after strange flesh." Recall in the story of Sodom and Gomorrah when the angels came to warn

Lot to get out of the city before the judgment of God, the men of Sodom wanted to have sex with (to "know") the angels in Lot's house. The men of Sodom wanted to "go after strange flesh" and just as the fallen angels suffer "the vengeance of eternal fire," in Lot's day, the vengeance of God upon Sodom and Gomorrah was FIRE as well. So that we see the Judgment of FIRE associated with the sin of "fornication, and going after strange flesh."

Fornication is *any* type of sexual activity outside of God's set boundaries of heterosexual intercourse within the bonds of matrimony. This includes heterosexual sex between unmarried people, homosexuality, bestiality, necromancy, pedophilia, and all types of perverted sexual behavior. According to the text of Jude, "strange flesh" seems to be not only homosexual sex, but also sex with non-human entities, such as fallen angels. The fallen angels of the Old Testament went after the "strange flesh" of human women, the men of Sodom wanted the "strange flesh" of the Holy Angels visiting Lot.

2 Peter 3:6-7 tells us, **"Whereby the world that then was, being overflowed with water, perished: But the heavens and the earth, which are now, by the same word are kept in store, reserved unto fire against the day of judgment and perdition of ungodly men."** Speaking of the time of God's fiery judgment upon the earth, John tells us in Revelation 9:21, "Neither repented they of their murders, nor of their sorceries, nor of their **fornication**, nor of their thefts."

(Could it be that the world-wide fascination with UFO's is really a flirtation with Satanic beings, fallen angels, who will seduce the world in the time of the end just as they did in the time before the flood as recorded in the Pseudepigrapha book of Enoch, which is directly quoted from in the book of Jude?) As the Lord said, the end times will be as the days of Noah!

AIDS:

"Free Love" of the 1970's brought the AIDS epidemic of the 1980's and by 1992, Acquired Immune Deficiency Syndrome was the leading cause of death among men ages 25 to 44 years in the USA. AIDS was easily traced back to the homosexual community and for the first decade of the outbreak, most of those who succumbed to AIDS related illnesses were homosexual males. In 1994, an obituary study revealed that the median age of death for homosexuals was age 42 for men and age 49 for women.(100) In fact, every form of sexually transmitted disease runs rampant in the homosexual community, with gay men having the highest incidence of syphilis in the USA of any other population group. They also suffer from health complications unique to their lifestyle such as "gay bowel syndrome".

Romans 1:21-32

"...when they knew God, they glorified him not as God, neither were thankful; but became vain in their imaginations, and their foolish heart was darkened.²² Professing themselves to be wise, they became fools,²³ And changed the glory of the uncorruptible God into an image made like to corruptible man, and to birds, and fourfooted beasts, and creeping things.²⁴ Wherefore God also gave them up to uncleanness through the lusts of their own hearts, to dishonour their own bodies between themselves:²⁵ Who changed the truth of God into a lie, and worshipped and served the creature more than the Creator, who is blessed for ever. Amen.[26] For this cause God gave them up unto vile affections: for even their women did change the natural use into that which is against nature: [27] And likewise also the men, leaving the natural use of the woman, burned in their lust one toward another; men with men working that which is unseemly, and receiving in themselves that recompence of their error which was meet.[28] And even as they did not like to retain God in their knowledge, God gave them over to a reprobate mind, to do those things which are not con- venient;[29] Being filled with all unrighteousness, fornication, wickedness, covetousness, maliciousness; full of envy, murder, debate, deceit, malignity; whisperers,[30] Backbiters, haters of God, despiteful, proud, boasters, inventors of evil things, disobedient to parents,[31] Without understanding, covenantbreakers, without natural affection, implacable, unmerciful:[32] Who knowing the judgment of God, that they which commit such things are worthy of death, not only do the same, but have pleasure in them that do them."

Satan is the master of deception. He comes as an angel of light to entice with seemingly beautiful fruit, but it is a poison apple he is offering. He wants to cut down, snuff out, and drag as many souls to Hell as he possibly can. But God loves us and wants the very best life for us. John 10:10 tells us, **"The thief cometh not, but for to steal, and to kill, and to destroy: I am come that they might have life, and that they might have it more abundantly."** Every enticement of the devil discussed in this chapter leads to sorrow and regret. **Romans 6:23, "For the wages of sin is death; but the gift of God is eternal life through Jesus Christ our Lord." Proverbs 16:25, "There is**

a way that seemeth right unto a man, but the end thereof are the ways of death."

God's plan for the building a Godly society that brings blessings, prosperity and love to the world was *the family*. God created men and woman to be different. They each have strengths and weaknesses which are complementary to each other. God planned for man and woman as husband and wife, to work together, to be a team. God intended for two to become one, a whole unit, a family. The decade of the 1950's seems to have been the last decade in which traditional ideas of marriage and family prevailed in the USA.

Having lived a total of 13 years outside the United States in Europe and the Philippines, I can tell you that the America of the 1950's is what the world looks up to as the gold standard of liberty, opportunity, and morality. Today, the USA is hated in many places. Why? It is not because of missionaries like me bringing the Good News of the Gospel to the world. The USA is the global leader in charitable organizations who finance and deliver aid to the hungry and needy all around the globe. But it is because the good being done is overshadowed by the evil of pornographic movies, money making wars, and the export of liberal ideology such as homosexual marriage.

In summary, the sexual revolution is still being hailed as a good thing by the world. But the truth is that every category of dreadful development which will bring in the kingdom of the Antichrist is considered good by the lost. If they remain lost, they will see the fruit of their efforts on the day the world peace plan is announced by the global leaders. Governments will surrender their countries to the ten-division (Revelation 17:12) New World Order headed by the Anti-Christ, the Beast, who will unite the world on that day, the first day of the Tribulation, for a 7 year period (Daniel 9:27).

Where will you be on that fateful day? Will you be in your mansion in heaven, preparing for the Marriage Supper of the Lamb with the rest of the true Church of the Lord Jesus Christ? What about your family? Are they caught in these sexual snares of Satan's seduction? Are they under his spell? Let us agree together in prayer that the spiritual scales which are blinding them from the Truth may fall from their eyes!

Heavenly Father,

We come before you in the Mighty Name of Jesus Christ! We ask you, Lord, to let Your Word of Luke 4:18-19, be fulfilled this day in the hearing of our lost family and friends. **"The Spirit of the Lord *is* upon me, because he hath anointed me to preach the gospel to the poor; he hath sent me to heal the brokenhearted, to preach deliverance to the captives, and recovering of sight to the blind, to set at liberty them that are bruised, To preach the acceptable year of the Lord."** We ask You to touch the hearts of our families, Lord, and use us, Your children, to bring them into Your Kingdom before it is too late. We need your help, Lord, for we can do nothing without you!

We pray in Jesus' Name,
Amen!

Chapter 6

SATAN'S SEEDS

Matthew 13:24-25: "Another parable put he forth unto them, saying, The kingdom of heaven is likened unto a man which sowed good seed in his field: But while men slept, his enemy came and sowed tares among the wheat, and went his way."

It should come as no surprise when evil people, appearing to be Christians, infiltrate the church. Our Lord Jesus Christ warned us in this text and others that the enemy, Satan, will plant his people among the genuine wheat, the true Church. They look like wheat (Christians), but they do not bear nourishing fruit. They are tares, weeds that bring forth a crop of toxic produce. Only at the End of the Church Age will they be separated. This chapter will examine some of the tares that the enemy has planted over the last 2000 years and consider how Satan's plan and the End Time Harvest are converging as we near the end of the age.

The great falling away, spoken of by the Apostle Paul, happening now, is one way to know that the Church Age is rapidly coming to a close. **2 Thessalonians 2:2-4 "That ye be not soon shaken in mind, or be troubled, neither by spirit, nor by word, nor by letter as from us, as that the day of Christ is at hand.[3] Let no man deceive you by any means: for that day shall not come, except there come a falling away first, and that man of sin be revealed, the son of perdition;[4] Who opposeth and exalteth himself above all that is called God, or that is worshipped; so that he as God sitteth in the temple of God, shewing himself that he is God."** Even though in 53 AD, the date scholars believe the book was written, Paul reassured his readers that the "day of Christ" was not yet near; today, 1960 years later, it certainly is. "Scoffers," as written by Peter, can now be found throughout the church. **2 Peter 3:3-4, "Knowing this first, that there shall come in the last days scoffers, walking after their own lusts,[4] And saying, Where is the promise of his coming? for since the fathers fell asleep, all things continue as they were from the beginning of the creation."** The unbelievers of the world have always scoffed. It would be redundant for the apostle Peter to tell his readers that pagans will make fun of them. Thus it must be the lukewarm, fallen-away Church which Peter had in mind in that text. He was looking ahead to the vast majority of churches that comprise Christendom today: churches that are just a show and a lukewarm, worldly, compromised mess.

The Book of Acts was written between 61 and 65 AD, and documents the persecution of early Christians beginning with the stoning of deacon Stephen, Christianity's first martyr, by zealous Jews. Saul of Tarsus, who would later become Paul, the apostle to the Gentiles, was a Pharisee who was heavily involved in the Jewish persecution of the newly formed Christian sect. But the persecution was not limited to the Jewish community. In 64 AD, the great fire of Rome was blamed upon the Christians by Emperor Nero, whom historians now almost unanimously agree was the arsonist. Persecution of Christians escalated until the end of the third to the beginning of the fourth century AD. During the "Great Persecution" under Emperor Diocletian, over 20,000 Christians were executed by the most gruesome means. Diocletian, who ruled Rome from 284 to 324, is most famous for feeding Christians to lions in the coliseums of the Empire. Although the Edict of Milan issued in the year 313 AD, officially ended Roman persecution of Christianity, but it did not actually become law for all of the empire until Christianity became the "official religion" in 380 AD, during the reign of Emperor Constantine.

The devil had tried everything to destroy the young Church. It had not worked, so as the saying goes, "If you can't beat 'em, join 'em." This is yet another example of a seemingly good thing—the ending of the most horrible period of Christian persecution the people of God had seen until that time—being distorted by Satan and used to corrupt the church of God. Constantine's declaration of Christianity as the official religion of the Roman Empire did not just bring the Christians out of their catacombs (where they had been worshipping in secret) but also started the process of integrating pagan customs and practices into Christian worship. The vigilant guard was let down. Christianity was now legal. Christians could come out of hiding and openly proclaim their faith. As the Lord said in the parable (Matthew 13:25); the enemy sowed weeds among the wheat while the workers slept. When the threat of persecution was lowered, Christians let down their guard and Satan slipped in to sow his seeds in the church—weed seeds.

Satan is the god of this world. **Luke 4:5-7**, recounts Satan's temptation of Jesus, **"And the devil, taking him up into an high mountain, shewed unto him all the kingdoms of the world in a moment of time.⁶ And the devil said unto him, All this power will I give thee, and the glory of them: for that is delivered unto me; and to whomsoever I will I give it.⁷ If thou therefore wilt worship me, all shall be thine."** Notice that Christ did not dispute Satan's claim because what the devil said was true, the kingdoms of the world do belong to him and he is able to manipulate them for his own means. Verse 8, **"And Jesus answered and said unto him, Get thee behind me, Satan: for it is written, Thou shalt worship the Lord thy God, and him only shalt thou serve."**

So, pagan Rome was declared Christian. By the stroke of the pen, Satan was given free access to the hierarchy of the Church. The Pantheon, the home of the gods, was merely changed from pagan to Christian without true conversion. The old pagan priests "converted" as the emperor commanded them. Even the Title "Pontifex Maximus", now used to denote the Pope of the Roman Catholic Church, was originally the terms used for the leader of the "College of Pontiffs", the highest ranking priests in the ancient Roman pagan religion.(101)

This is not to say that Roman Catholics, as individuals, are evil. Many may even be unaware of how early on in the history of the church Satan began to infiltrate the ranks of leadership, and bit by bit proceeded to transform the Book of Acts move of God that identified early Christianity into a "religious system."

We would also add that there are many Catholics who love the Lord and are Born Again believers, who are saved despite the teachings of the Roman Catholic Church. Just as there are in Evangelical Churches many people who have never been Born Again, who are not saved. Salvation is a personal, individual experience, between each specific believer and Jesus Christ. We are saved by grace, through (our individual) faith. Every instance of conversion in the New Testament involved individuals, not groups. For example as Jesus passed by Jericho, which was a corrupt city, a great crowd of people thronged him. Yet Jesus came to eat with only one of them, Zacchaeus "And when they saw it, they all murmured, saying, that he was gone to be guest with a man that is a sinner." (Luke 19:7) Jesus said to him, "This day is salvation come to *this house.*" Everyone in the crowd was in the presence of Jesus that day, yet Salvation only came to one individual, Zacchaeus.

The real problem I have encountered in over 13 years of ministry is that people are hiding from the Lord. Whether they may be hiding behind rituals and ceremonies that they believe can bridge the gap between them and God, or hiding behind a Godly spouse. Usually this is a husband hiding behind his wife because, as statistics show, over 60% of church attendees are women. This presents many problems within congregations for the devil to exploit. The so called "Jezebel spirit" has a way of rising in churches which lack strong male role models for the younger members, especially if those churches also have weak pastors. That spirit comes from Satan who is the master of manipulation and of turning good situations (lots of women in church) into bad ones. The "Jezebel spirit" is sent to try and knock out the pastor and male church leaders by any means necessary, just as Jezebel of the Old Testament used everything within her power to put down the prophet of God, that same spirit is at work in the church today to divide and destroy the church. Satan puts fear into the heart of the pastor so that he can be manipulated and even seduced into sin. This is just one way in which Satan is working to kill, steal, and destroy God's people. But, the devil would also use this to try to blame women for problems in the church which are actually be traced to the fact that men are absent from their roles as leaders of the family and the church. We must be alert as 1 Peter 5:8 tells us, **"Be sober, be vigilant; because your adversary the devil, as a roaring lion, walketh about, seeking whom he may devour"**

For the sake of time, we can visualize the church from Pentecost to the present day as a line graph.

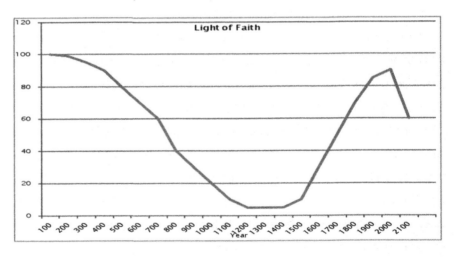

The church began with maximum light, walking in the will of the Lord. It slowly dimmed until it reached a low point during the dark ages. In the past 500 years, as the End Times began approaching, the Holy Spirit is being poured out once again as it was in the beginning, in Acts 2, to prepare the church for the "fullness of times", as we mentioned in the beginning of this book. Martin Luther received the revelation from the Lord, "the just shall live by faith." The Holy Spirit began from that time to increase the Light of the Gospel in the world.

When St. Jerome began translating the Bible into Latin in 382 AD (a project that took until 405 AD to complete), Latin was the common language of the western world, having replaced Greek as the language of the people due to the influence of imperial Rome. But, as Rome declined and was invaded by other people groups, Latin developed into what we now know as Romance Languages or was replaced by the languages of invading Germanic tribes. The result was that by the 9th Century AD, (mid 800's), Latin was no longer understood by any but the educated (kings and clergy). Yet it continued to be used as the language of international communication, scholarship, and science until well into the 18th century. It also continued to be used by the Church.(102)

According to History books, the "dark ages" are so named because of the cultural and economic deterioration and disruption that occurred in Europe following the decline of the Roman Empire. War and destruction caused by (pagan) barbarian Goths, Vandals, and Huns that swept down on Europe from the north and east, resulted in the burning and plundering Roman art and architecture. One result of this mayhem and madness was that during this period most people did not learn to read or write, thus the "lamp of learning" burned dimly.

As a consequence, during this time people were going to Mass but were hearing the Bible read and the prayers prayed in a language that was not spoken anywhere outside the church walls. Only those who were wealthy enough to receive an education could read the Bible for themselves. And since the printing press was not invented until the 1400's, Bibles were very scarce. After all, they had to be copied by hand, in daylight hours (or by candlelight), a process that would take up to forty years.(103) Even though monasteries around the world were making manuscripts of the Bible at all times, there were rarely enough to go around. So only the richest parishes had their own copies. These Bibles were priceless treasures, representing one man's lifetime of work, and as such would be chained to the parish pulpits.

People who could not read for themselves and who could not understand the language of the scriptures being read to them in church, did not know that Salvation comes by grace through faith. They only knew what they were told, which was that salvation came through ceremonies, called sacraments. These sacraments could only be administered by priests of the Roman Catholic Church. So, apart from the Church was no chance of Heaven. Even the educated and wealthy believed that the Church held the "keys to the kingdom" (Matthew 16:19, "And I will give unto thee the keys of the kingdom of heaven: and whatsoever thou shalt bind on earth shall be bound in heaven: and whatsoever thou shalt loose on earth shall be loosed in heaven."), so that excommunication was the greatest threat—without communion with the church, people believed they could not go to Heaven. In fact, King Henry IV of the Holy Roman Empire in the year 1077 was forced to stand barefoot in the snow outside of the Pope's palace for three days, as penance so that he could receive absolution (forgiveness of sins). Henry not only stood barefoot, but he fasted and wore a haircloth shirt to increase his sufferings. When Pope Gregory finally let him in, Henry knelt before him and begged forgiveness so that he could be received back into the church. (He was "un-excommunicated" and that evening Pope Gregory, King Henry and his wife Matilda shared communion.)(104)

Of course we all remember from history that during the Renaissance, the Roman Catholic Church censored scientists who published any findings that might cast doubt upon the Church's world view. The astronomer, Galileo, caused quite a controversy with his discovery that the earth (and all the planets) revolves around the sun. This heliocentric view of the universe cause such turmoil within the Church that he was called to appear before the Roman Inquisition in 1615. It is interesting to note that he had been defended by Jesuit lawyers until he published, *Dialogue between the Two Chief world Systems,* which appeared to attack Pope. With the Jesuits no longer representing him, he was tried by the Inquisition and found "vehemently suspect of heresy".(105) The Church forced him to recant, placed him under house arrest, and left him there for the rest of his life.

Ironically, the Roman Catholic Church is leading the way in star gazing now! And once again the counter-reformation order, also known as the Jesuits, or Society of Jesus, is right in the middle of it. Although the First Vatican Counsel, 1869, had this to say about Darwin's Theory of Evolution: "If anyone does not confess that the world and all things which are contained in it, both spiritual and material, were produced, according to their whole substance, out of nothing by God; or holds that God did not create by his will free from all necessity, but as necessarily as he necessarily loves himself; or denies that the world was created for the glory of God: let him be anathema." (106) The Roman Catholic Church has now moved to a position commonly known as "Theistic Evolution" (sometimes called "evolutionary creation"). In 1996, Pope John Paul II said, "Today, new findings lead us toward the recognition of evolution as more than a hypothesis. In fact it is remarkable that this theory has had progressively greater influence on the spirit of researchers, following a series of discoveries in different scholarly disciplines. The convergence in the results of these independent studies—which was neither planned nor sought—constitutes in itself a significant argument in favor of the theory." which sounds a lot like an endorsement of evolution except in regards to the origin of the human soul, "Theories of evolution which, because of the philosophies which inspire them, regard the spirit either as emerging from the forces of living matter, or as a simple epiphenomenon of that matter, are incompatible with the truth about man."(107) The Vatican's top astronomer, Rev. Jose Gabriel Funes, director of the Vatican Observatory, was quoted in L'Osservatore Romano, the Vatican's official newspaper, "Just as a multiplicity of creatures exists on the Earth, so there could be other creatures, even intelligent ones, created by God," the Argentine Jesuit said. "This does not conflict with our faith, because we cannot set limits on the creative liberty of God." He went on to further comment, "It is not a given that they have need of redemption," he said. "They may have remained in full friendship with their Creator."(108) In other words, aliens might be real and they may have a better Gospel!

The Lord began to restore the End Times Church in the days of Martin Luther. We say, "end times", because a day with the Lord is like 1000 years to us. **(But, beloved, be not ignorant of**

this one thing, that one day is with the Lord as a thousand years, and a thousand years as one day. 2 Peter 3:8) God does things over what we humans perceive as long periods of time. So, the lights went up little by little, as the Lord pushed back the darkness, to restore one doctrine and a time. The graph began to move up from the lowest point. This restoration has been growing ever since that time, as the Lord has restored truth and light to His true church throughout the 500 + years since 1517 when Martin Luther posted his Ninety-Five Thesis on the door of the Church in Wittenberg, Saxony.

Let's look at a few examples, to get an idea of where this river of reformation is flowing:

The 1524 Anabaptist movement was the first to reject infant Baptism. The name *Anabaptist* is from the Greek words, "*ana baptista*", meaning "one who baptizes over again." The name was actually given to them by their enemies who took issue with the practice of "re-baptizing" converts who already had been baptized as infants by sprinkling. But, history, Archeology, and study of Greek etymology would prove the Anabaptists had a good understanding of scripture on this issue. Following rabbinical regulations requiring immersion of the whole body, referred to as *tevilah*, John the Baptist certainly would have baptized by immersion in "living water" (a Hebrew idiomatic expression meaning flowing water) either by using a natural stream, such as the Jordan River, or by using a mikveh (a specially constructed ritual bath, connected directly to a natural source of water, such as a spring).(109)

Archeological evidence has revealed ancient churches all over Asia Minor (modern day Turkey) and the Mediterranean coast with baptisteries built in the style of the Jewish mikveh.

141

So we now know that all baptism was by immersion until the 1300's, and the Eastern Rite churches still baptize by immersion (they immerse infants as well as adult converts). The Greek words used in the original text of the New Testament, βαπτιζω (baptizo = baptise) and βαπτισμα (baptisma = baptism) mean to *"make whelmed"* (which is an archaic English word that means *fully wet,* or *washed,* the closest cognate in modern English is "overwhelmed"). This Greek word is used only in the New Testament to mean ceremonial *ablution,* especially that of the ordinance of Christian *baptism.* **"Therefore we are buried with him by baptism into death: that like as Christ was raised up from the dead by the glory of the Father, even so we also should walk in newness of life." Romans 6:4.** The whole western church was blinded by the devil to the simple understanding of the plain meaning of the Word of God (and the Greek word, βαπτιζω)! The restoration of this truth was revolutionary in its time, and contrary to accepted beliefs, so that "the old guard" of religion fought it with all their might.

Isaiah 28:10, "For precept must be upon precept, precept upon precept; line upon line, line upon line; here a little, and there a little" Martin Luther received the revelation of "The Just Shall Live by Faith" but he did not embrace the notion of Baptism by immersion that the Anabaptists were promoting. Each restoration resulted in a new denomination, Lutherans (1517), Calvinist-Anabaptists(1555), Presbyterians (1560)

More revelation would come to a new, on-fire generation, like Holiness living with John Wesley (founder of the Methodist Church). On May 24, 1738, John Wesley had an experience that would be life-changing, he wrote of it in his journal, saying, "In the evening, I went very unwillingly to a society in Aldersgate

Street, where one was reading Luther's preface to the Epistle to the Romans. About a quarter before nine, while he was describing the change which God works in the heart through faith in Christ, I felt my heart strangely warmed. I felt I did trust in Christ, Christ alone for salvation, and an assurance was given me that he had taken away my sins, even mine, and saved me from the law of sin and death."(110) John Wesley came away from that meeting with a new zeal and fire for living a holy life before God. Even though God had used Martin Luther's words to stir the heart of John Wesley, the former reformers, would be used by the devil to persecute the "new teachings."

The Anglican Church, in which Wesley was ordained and which he wanted to reform, became so perturbed by his preaching on holiness of heart and life that they banned him from their churches, calling his "Methodism" a cult. From then on Wesley preached wherever an assembly could be brought together, in churches when he was invited, in the fields, halls, cottages, and chapels when the church would not receive him. On more than one occasion, he used his father's tombstone at Epworth as his pulpit. Wesley continued his preaching of holiness as God's standard of living for His people for fifty years.(111) John Wesley and the Methodist movement were at the vanguard of the First Great Awakening of 1730–1760 which challenged the rituals, piety and self awareness of established Protestant churches of the day.(112)

Unbelievably, after a time of growth and formation, the holiness movement of Methodism took on the role of the "religious establishment" so when the Pentecostal movement hit at Azusa Street in 1906, the holiness people were the very first to condemn the new movement. The irony is that the Wesleyan-holiness heritage is what distinguished Pentecostalism. Acts 5:32 tells us that God gives the Holy Spirit "to those who obey Him." So it was a natural thing for those who were seeking God and striving to live holy lives should receive the Gift of the Holy Spirit. **Jeremiah 29:10, "And ye shall seek me, and find me, when ye shall search for me with all your heart**." Although Pentecostalism was an outgrowth of the holiness movement, it was persecuted by the very group from which it sprang.

Simply put, the Lord answers the cries of the few who seriously seek Him and sends revival. Through that revival, more truth is restored to the body of Christ. It is like the video and song by Carman, *Revival in the Land*. When the Lord is pouring out His Spirit, the devil is thrown into fear and confusion. The enemy is scattered. The revival group advances the Kingdom of the Lord and huge numbers of that generation are swept into the Kingdom.

The preachers of these great revivals were nobodies. Outsiders. Not in the religious clique. Though they may have been ordained in a certain denomination (Luther was a Catholic priest, Wesley was an Anglican cleric), they were not high up in their religious organizations. Then, out of their teaching and the move of God which followed, a denomination would form and from there, things begin to formalize. A hierarchy would be established to control who could be leaders and ministers in the group. The leadership then begins to require formal education to preach the Gospel. Go to their school, where they will teach the Bible as they understand it. First, 2 years, then 4 years are required. Then a Master's degree or a PhD is necessary to be a big "somebody" in the group. The enemy sows his religious people among the true servants of the Lord in the movement, as it is established. The revival of the Lord then becomes "mainstream" Christianity. Once that happens, the World thinks the group is "okay," and not "wacky" or too extreme.

Now the devil's people, who have gotten the church leadership under their spell, whisper, "lets not offend anyone. Let's mix a little water with the blood." Then, little by little, the group falls away from the truth, and into the arms of this world, of which Satan is the god as 2 Corinthians 4:4 says, **"In whom the <u>god of this world</u> hath blinded the minds of them which believe not, lest the light of the glorious gospel of Christ, who is the image of God, should shine unto them."**

One of the greatest examples of this watering down of the Gospel ahs happened in the Methodist church. Methodism, started by that mighty man of God John Wesley, was born in the holiness movement of the mid-1700's, and was the group that lead the way in the great revival that swept through the Untied States of America during the "Second Great Awakening". Yet this group which was once on the forefront of a great move of God that won millions to the Kingdom of Heaven has sadly decided to "mix a little water with the blood," and more. As long ago as 1989, the United Methodist Publishing House began to "transition" their hymnals so that today, literally ALL hymns that mention the Blood of our Lord Jesus Christ have been removed so as not to offend the devil and his weeds! (113)

The movement that led the First and Second Great Awakenings in the United States sparked the term "Holy Rollers", a disparaging moniker mocking the thousands that fell and rolled on the ground under the convicting power of the Holy Spirit during those powerful calls to holiness and repentance by John Wesley, Jonathan Edwards and George

Whitfield (First Great Awakening, 1730-1750), and in the next generation, Charles Finney, Richard Allen and Peter Cartwright (Second Great Awakening 1780-1810). This is the group that gave us the open air crusades and tent revivals, used even today by Billy Graham and others. Yet the very denominations which were on the vanguard of the First and Second Great Awakening—Methodist, Presbyterian and Congregationalists for the most part—are now religious institutions that require a master's degree to preach and whose sermons come from the central authority of their "common liturgy" instead of from the Lord to each pastor. Dead tradition. This is the devil's doing, and it is an abomination in our eyes.

Today, much worse than simply falling away from holiness to lukewarm, tasteless salt has affected the Christian Church around the world. A new wave of anti-Semitism has arisen in the Lutheran, Episcopal (Church of England), and other denominations termed "theological anti-Semitism." Worse still, there are even some protestant groups with gay bishops who left their wives and children to marry another man. The United Church of Christ was the first to perform same-sex marriages(114) followed by Unitarian Universalists and Episcopals. The Episcopal Church (USA) consecrated its first gay Bishop in 2003 (115) and its first lesbian Bishop (diocese of Los Angeles) in 2010. (116) The issue of gay clergy has been so divisive for the Episcopal Church that not only have individual congregations world-wide broken ties with the denomination, but the entire delegation of Nigerian Anglican Bishops have threatened to split off from the Church of England because of it. (117) The Evangelical Lutheran Church of America, the largest and most "progressive" Lutheran synod in America, since 2009 both recognizes and performs same-sex marriage and allows openly gay and lesbian pastors. (118)

Still more shocking is the willingness to compromise the Gospel in exchange for political correctness. Saddleback Church of Lake Forrest, California, with its famous pastor, Rick Warrens, is promoting Islam through its "good neighbor program" which is designed to increase understanding between Christians and Muslims that in Warrens' own words is "out of 'Love Thy Neighbor,' not focused on conversion." (119) On June 26, 2011, 130 Churches from various denominations across the United States held "Shared Faith" events in which Muslim clerics were invited to read from the Quran during worship services to promote the unity of Christianity and Islam, called "Chrislam."(120)

And now there are "Muslim-friendly Bibles!" That's right. Wycliffe Bible Translators, the Summer Institute of Linguistics (SIL) and Frontiers are all producing Bible translations that remove or change terminology which could be "offensive" to Muslims. This includes the removal of references to God as "Father" and Jesus as "Son" or "Son of God." For example, in one the new Arabic versions of the Gospel of Matthew from Frontiers and SIL, Matthew 28:19, "baptizing them in the name of the Father and the Son and the Holy Spirit" is changed to "cleanse them by water in the name of Allah, his Messiah and his Holy Spirit." It remains to be seen if the outcry from evangelical missionaries and many former Muslim converts from countries where these Bible translations are being used will have any effect on this watering down of the Gospel. (121)

Statistics paint a distressing portrait of post-modern Christendom. A 1998 poll of 7,441 Protestant clergy in the

U.S.A. showed that 19% of Lutherans, 34% of Baptists, 44% of Episcopalians, 49% of Presbyterians, and 60% of Methodists do NOT BELIEVE IN THE VIRGIN BIRTH OF JESUS CHRIST! A similar poll conducted in the United Kingdom in 2000 showed that 25% of Catholic priests and 47% of Church of England Priests in that country do not believe in the Virgin Birth.(122) It seems the whole church has fallen away! No wonder our Lord asked, **"When the Son of man cometh, shall he find faith on the earth?"** (Luke 18:8b)

One result of the lowering of standards and the spirit of compromise that has infiltrated the churches is a huge reduction in church attendance. When there is no difference between the church and the world, people will choose the world. In 1955, 45% of Protestants and 75% of Catholics attended church weekly. Recent polls now indicate that Protestant church attendance has dropped slightly to about 40%, and Catholics have declined significantly to 45%. But the poll data is compared to church attendance records (like the chart on page 173) one can see that only about 1/2 the people who say they are going to church each week really are. When the number of people claiming to be mainline Protestant, Evangelical and Roman Catholic is compared to the attendance records of the churches, pollsters conclude that real attendance is between 17-20%! (123)

Going to church does not make you a Christian any more than going to McDonalds makes you a cheeseburger. But at church Christians are discipled! Discipleship is the process of growing in the Lord, learning to bear fruit and be salt and light. The baby boomers were taken to church in huge numbers. Most of them heard the Gospel and know the truth, whether they are saved or not. But the baby boomers dropped out of church en mass as young adults. As a result, their children have never been to church or heard the Gospel. **Romans 10:14, "How then shall they call on him in whom they have not believed? and how shall they believe in him of whom they have not heard? and how shall they hear without a preacher?"**

Here in the Philippines, and many developing countries, there is something called folk religion. The people of the world are seeking help. Supernatural help. They have little money, and the medical system is lacking in standards. But, the Church is not a well know option, because of the lack of mature, Spirit-filled Christians. So, people turn to the witch doctors or "spirit men" for help. These witch doctors, of course, have supernatural powers, like Simon the Sorcerer in Acts 8. That power is not from the Lord, but the devil! Many Western Christians no longer believe in the power of evil spirits, they explain away spiritual phenomenon as "mind over matter." But evil is very real! (I have cast the demons out of dozens who were under the power of these witch doctors here in the Philippines! I could write a book just on that!)

So, too, since the 1950's, we have seen an explosion of New Age spiritualist, mediums, and Wicca (which is witchcraft). The spiritual void left in the West by the backslidden Church is being filled by television shows and book series with themes of sorcery and witchcraft.

This spiral of declining church attendance can be reversed! And this is the heart of this book, and my calling: WE DO NOT NEED MIDDLE AGED PREACHERS DRESSING "COOL", WEARING EARRINGS AND TALKING NARLY TO MAKE THE GOSPEL RELAVANT TO THIS GENERATION!

Zachariah 4:6, "Not by might, nor by power, but by my spirit, saith the Lord of hosts." We DO NOT need to win people to ourselves, or a church (denomination), we need to lead them to JESUS! He is the one who saves! He is the Captain of Our Salvation! **(Hebrews 2:10, "For it became him, for whom are all things, and by whom are all things, in bringing many sons unto glory, to make the captain of their salvation perfect through sufferings.")**

This author strongly urges anyone who is weak in the faith to flee those churches which are teaching another Gospel. **"But though we, or an angel from heaven, preach any other gospel unto you than that which we have preached unto you, let him be accursed." Galatians 1:8.** If you are strong and mature in the faith, may you be bold to speak the truth in your church. May you rise up and answer the call of a watchman! Warn the people, trouble is coming! The wrath of the Lord is coming; it is even at the door! Flee the world; come out of this world, for it shall perish with all who love it, in a moment. For the Lord will come at a moment, and an hour you least expect!

"For the Lord Himself shall descend from heaven with a shout, with the voice of the archangel, and with the trump of God: and the dead in Christ shall rise first" 1 Thessalonians 4:16

"In a moment, in the twinkling of an eye, at the last trump: for the trumpet shall sound, and the dead shall be raised incorruptible, and we shall be changed." 1 Corinthians 15:52

Needless to say, not even the darkest days of the past will be anything like the darkness of the Tribulation to come. The

Lord will allow Satan to wield such power during the time after the Rapture of the Church that the Dark Ages will seem like Heaven on earth.

At the beginning of this book, the "fullness of time" was discussed. The Lord has a predetermined timeframe in which to carry out His plans. From the fullness of evil that will be allowed while His Bride is on earth to the fullness of the Gentiles who will come to the saving knowledge of our Lord Jesus Christ, the "fullness of time" is almost here. Just as the Lord told Abraham that He would bring the children of Israel out of Bondage to bring His judgment of the people's who lived in Canaan, when the "iniquity of the Amorites" had reach it fullness. (Genesis 15:15), Satan's chalice of sins in our world today is filling fast. Since beginning to write this book in May of 2013, there have been daily headlines proving that the world is waxing worse and worse just as 2 Timothy 3:13 says, **"But evil men and seducers shall wax worse and worse, deceiving, and being deceived."** In fact events are happening at such an increasingly rapid pace that staying current with the headlines as this book is being written has become almost impossible. To keep adding in the latest move in Satan's game plan would result in this book never being finished or published! The world is much worse now than just those few months ago. Time is short!

In John 7:7, the Lord Jesus Christ, speaking to his relatives who did not believe that He was the Messiah, said, **"Then Jesus said unto them, My time is not yet come: but your time is always ready. The world cannot hate you; but me it hateth, because I testify of it, that the works thereof are evil."** James 4:4 tells us, **"whosoever therefore will be a friend of the world is the enemy of God."** So, the enemy

(Satan) and his people want the world to love them, for they are of the world. But 1 John 2:15 tells us, **"Love not the world, neither the things that are in the world. If any man love the world, the love of the Father is not in him."** But of the true church the Lord said, **"If ye were of the world, the world would love his own: but because ye are not of the world, but I have chosen you out of the world, therefore the world hateth you." (John 15:19)** We are hated by the world, if we are truly walking in the pilgrim way. We are not citizens of this world, which is passing away, but we are pilgrims traveling through this earth as a strangers on our way to a city **"whose builder and maker is God,"** (Hebrews 11:10) our true home in heaven with our Lord and Master, Jesus Christ.

The message of this chapter is that America can be revived. The Lord can send a mighty End Times Harvest! **2 Chronicles 7:14, "If my people, which are called by my name, shall humble themselves, and pray, and seek my face, and turn from their wicked ways; then will I hear from heaven, and will forgive their sin, and will heal their land."** We do not need religion, we need Jesus! Religion is man's attempt to prevent people from coming to God by imposing rules and regulations instead of allowing them to go straight to God our Father through Jesus Christ. **Hebrews 4:16, "Let us therefore come boldly unto the throne of grace that we may obtain mercy, and find grace to help in time of need."**

The Lord is restoring truth to His church. From Martin Luther to Azusa Street, each move of God has added to the restoration and moved the church closer and closer to the original book of Acts model New Testament Christianity. Revival comes to those who are willing to ignore tradition and seek Him in Spirit and Truth, as Jesus told the Samaritan woman at the well, John 4:23, **"But the hour cometh, and now is, when the true worshippers shall worship the Father in spirit and in truth: for the Father seeketh such to worship him."** Some traditions are fine, but others become a substitute for building a genuine relationship with Jesus Christ. For example, many people go to churches with pre-planned programs or elaborate ceremonies which are consistently predictable from Sunday to Sunday. Man-made religious ceremonies make them feel comfortable. Others may not attend formal churches that follow a liturgy, but they still become irritated if Sunday morning worship lasts past 12:00 noon, or if the worship leader sings more than three songs, or repeats the chorus more than once.

What if God wishes to move in a way that doesn't fit the man-made order of the service? Or what if the Lord does not really desire the worship in song to be separated from the preaching by grinning announcements of the youth barbeque fundraiser? What if the Jesus wants the entire congregation to come forward to the altar in repentance and prayer for two hours? Or three? Or four? Most churches would not allow God to change their schedules because most church people are hiding from the Lord in their comfortable religious practices. They do not really know Jesus and He does not know them.

This is why very few churches in the western world are operating in the power of the Holy Spirit. This is why the church has falling into greater and greater darkness. This is how the American church has reached the place where the bells of the National Cathedral are rung in celebration of the Supreme Court's decision to overturn laws that ban gay marriage! This has happened because the Church in the West, and particularly the USA, has become lukewarm. Luke 12:48b, **"For unto whomsoever much is given, of him shall be much required: and to whom men have committed much, of him they will ask the more."** The USA has been blessed of God like no other country in history. Yet, the Church has dried up and withered, being disconnected from the True Vine. Everyone, has gone his own way, and has done what was right in his *own* eyes. (Judges 21:25. **"Every man did that which was right in his own eyes."**) Most people have forsaken the Lord. Now the Western Church is in free fall—a free falling away from the Lord and His Word. There is, and has already been, a great falling away within the Church. In every generation, Satan has sowed tares among the wheat. Yet that does not negate the calling of the Church of Jesus Christ to obey His command, "Occupy until I come" (Luke 19:13) and to be salt and light until the Rapture.

Religion is never the source of revival. Just as the Pharisees of the New Testament opposed Jesus, institutional religious systems always oppose the move of God. But the Lord has given us what we need for revival, as Jesus said, **"If ye have faith as a grain of mustard seed, ye shall say unto this mountain, Remove hence to yonder place; and it shall remove; and nothing shall be impossible unto you." (Matthew 17:20)** God will honor faith! Ask! Seek! Knock! **"Ask, and it shall be given you; seek, and ye shall find; knock, and it shall be opened unto you" (Matthew 7:7)** The Church does face mountains—big, imposing ones. But God is a mountain mover!

"And I sought for a man among them, that should make up the hedge, and stand in the gap before Me for the land, that I should not destroy it: but I found none." Ezekiel

22:30. God forbid that this be said of the Church of the living God today! Not at this critical hour. We, the Church must lead the way. **"If my people, which are called by my name, shall humble themselves, and pray, and seek my face, and turn from their wicked ways; then will I hear from heaven, and will forgive their sin, and will heal their land." 2 Chronicles 7:14.** We, the Church must take a stand and "Stand therefore!" **"Wherefore take unto you the whole armour of God, that ye may be able to withstand in the evil day, and having done all, to stand, Stand therefore" Ephesians 6:13-14(a)** It is time for the church to stand up against the giant in our land! Not through politics—**Zechariah4:6(b), "Not by might, nor by power, but by my spirit, saith the Lord of hosts."** —but by His Spirit!

The giant of the homosexual agenda would fall if such a revival swept the land that gays and lesbians would be radically transformed by the power of the Holy Spirit. What the Supreme Court does is meaningless. If all the lesbians, gays, bisexuals, and transgender (LGBT) people get saved and delivered, it would not matter what sort of marriage laws are on the books. The giant of the abortion industry would fall if the church reached out to abortion doctors with the life-changing message of the Gospel of Jesus Christ (rather than shooting doctors and picketing clinics). It does not matter what man does; only what God does! It only matters what God is doing in the hearts and lives of people. There are more with us than against us! When men and women, boys and girls are radically saved, walking in holiness and baptized "with the Holy Ghost, and with fire" spoken of by John the Baptist in Matthew 3:11, the giants will fall.

Psalm 85:6-7, "Wilt thou not revive us again: that thy people may rejoice in thee? Shew us thy mercy, O LORD, and grant us thy salvation."

Dear Heavenly Father,
I pray that You would revive my heart, O Lord, so that I can be used for Your glory to fill the gap, to be salt and light, and bring souls into Your Kingdom while there is still time. Here am I, Lord, send me! Let you will be done in my life, as it is in Heaven.

In Jesus' Name,
Amen!

Chapter 7

URGENT WARNING FOR AMERICA

Jeremiah 29:11 "For I know the plans I have for you," declares the Lord, "plans to prosper you and not to harm you, plans to give you hope and a future."

There are two ways to look at the world: the way Satan sees it or the way God sees it. The devil wants everyone, even Christians, to see the world his way. If the devil can convince the people of God to see through his set of binoculars, he knows they will miss what God is trying to do. Satan will even use the nearness of the Coming of Our Lord Jesus Christ to get us to veer off course and forget our mission. The enemy wants the church to be so focused on checking the skies for the Rapture that we sit down, shut and just keep looking up! But the Lord wants to bring revival!

Ephesians 4:14, "That we henceforth be no more children, tossed to and fro, and carried about with every wind of

doctrine, by the sleight of men, and cunning craftiness, whereby they lie in wait to deceive"

Many Christians are running back and forth, flipping through the channels so to speak, looking for the most sensational theory about when the Rapture will be. I myself have had dreams about the rapture, and of course if we know that someone is having dreams and visions that are coming to pass, we can put more weight in those; but no one's dream or vision supersedes the Bible. We have a SURE Word, the Word of God. Anything that contradicts the Word of God is *not* of God.

When the children of Israel worshipped the golden calf, God was angry with them. **Exodus 32:9-10, "And the Lord said unto Moses, I have seen this people, and, behold, it is a stiffnecked people. Now therefore let me alone, that my wrath may wax hot against them, and that I may consume them: and I will make of thee a great nation."** Moses interceded for them. **Exodus 32:13, "Remember Abraham, Isaac, and Israel, thy servants, to whom thou swarest by thine own self, and saidst unto them, I will multiply your seed as the stars of heaven, and all this land that I have spoken of will I give unto your seed, and they shall inherit it forever."** Of course God knew that Moses was going to pray for them and God already knew what He was going to do, but the Bible was written so we can understand. **Exodus 32:14, "And the Lord repented of the evil which He thought to do unto His people"** God changed his mind. In the same way, Abraham interceded for Sodom & Gomorrah asking the Lord to spare the city for the sake of 50, then 40, all the way down to 10 righteous souls. Then God said, "No, if I can find 10, I won't destroy it" (**Genesis 18:32, "And he said, Oh let not the Lord be angry, and I will speak yet but this once: Peradventure ten shall be found there. And he said, I will not destroy it for ten's sake."**)

There are certainly more than 10 righteous in the United States!

The disciples of our Lord Jesus also had a problem seeing the world the way Christ does. For example, the Sons of Thunder in the Gospel of Luke asked Jesus, "do you want us to call down fire from heaven on the town" (**Luke 9:54, "And when his disciples James and John saw this, they said, Lord, wilt thou that we command fire to come down from heaven, and consume them, even as Elias did?"**) and Jesus said, "you don't know what spirit you are of" (**Luke 9:55-56, "But he turned, and rebuked them, and said, Ye know not what manner of spirit ye are of. For the Son of man is not come to destroy men's lives, but to save them. And they went to another village."**) Even in the Old Testament, God did not destroy a people until the fullness of their sins had come up before His Face. Jesus did not come to destroy people, or to call down fire from heaven onto people, but he came that the world through Him might be saved. (**John 3:17, "For God sent not his Son into the world to condemn the world; but that the world through him might be saved."**)

Jesus came to *give* life—Abundant Life—to save the lost, yet so many in the United States (from local pulpits, on YouTube channels, and on internet websites) are preaching judgment, judgment, and more judgment. That is not Jesus' message! This is how HE sees the world: **John 3:16 "For God so loved the**

world, that he gave his only begotten Son, that whosoever believeth in him should not perish, but have everlasting life."

God *loves* the world and wants everyone to be saved. Yes, those who reject God will be judged; but their judgment will happen only when the fullness of their sins come up before God. And only, only, only God determines when His judgment will occur. We are not yet in the Tribulation. We are still in the Age of Grace. Condemnation and fear is not the message God has for His people, the Bride of Christ. **"But God has not given us the spirit of fear but of power, love & a sound mind."** (2 Timothy1:7) **"Let this mind be in you which was in Christ Jesus"**, (Philippians 2:5) He humbled himself even to the cross. **(Philippians 2:8, "And being found in fashion as a man, he humbled himself, and became obedient unto death, even the death of the cross.")**

God has used the Church in United States of America for over 200 years as a conduit of His grace and blessing, of His Holy Spirit outpouring into the world—that's why America is a blessed nation. America has spread the Gospel of Jesus Christ. Bibles are being translated into native languages of people all over the world by *Americans*. All of the Bibles in Philippines have been translated by Americans. It is Americans who go to third world countries, learn the native dialects and translate the Bible from the English into the local languages. There are no Hebrew or Greek scholars from the Philippines translating the Bible from the original languages to the Philippine languages. Americans translate them from English versions.

Where the Spirit of the Lord is there is liberty! (2 Corinthians 3:17) That Statue of Liberty represents freedom to the people of the world. When people of third-world countries, like the

Philippines, see that statue, they don't see Babylon, Apollyon, or corruption, they see a beacon of hope for those who yearn to be free! "Give me your tired huddled masses yearning to be free!" Freedom comes from God! It comes from Jehovah/ Yahweh the God of the Bible, the Lord God Almighty; the "I AM". *No other god* has the power to set the captives free. There is not one Muslim country in this world that has a governmental system even close to democracy, except Indonesia. Indonesia is only able to have a semi-democratic system because it is so far from the cradle of Satanic Islam. No other Muslim countries are democracies or representative republics.

America still has a constitution which grants freedom to her people. True freedom to be blessed and to bless others has only come to America because of Christianity, because of it has been founded on Christian principles. Yes, the United States has done bad things such as promoting pornography around the world. Yet the United States has more inventors than any other country. Americans invented the movie camera, the telephone, the computer, the internet, the cell phone, the radio, TV, all the technology we used was invented in USA—and many of those inventers were from other parts of the world who had come to America for freedom. **Luke 4: 18-19, "The Spirit of the Lord is upon me, because he hath anointed me to preach the gospel to the poor; he hath sent me to heal the brokenhearted, to preach deliverance to the captives, and recovering of sight to the blind, to set at liberty them that are bruised, To preach the acceptable year of the Lord."** There is no freedom in Satan, the devil comes to steal, kill & destroy, but Jesus came to give abundant life and liberty (John 10:10).

Luke 13:15-16, "The Lord then answered him, and said, Thou hypocrite, doth not each one of you on the sabbath loose his ox or his ass from the stall, and lead him away to watering? And ought not this woman, being a daughter of Abraham, whom Satan hath bound, lo, these eighteen years, be loosed from this bond on the sabbath day?" Satan had bound the woman in this passage with illness. And Satan has bound entire countries around the world by dictatorships and tyranny. Oppressive Government is of the devil. A Representative Republic can only flourish in a Christian nation with Christianity as its God-ordained foundation.

I believe that God sees the USA as beacon of liberty. The people of God need to stop listening to the devil who is saying that the USA is an evil place. Stop looking at the negative and focusing on evil! Start looking at the good and seeing things through God's eyes. **"Finally, brethren, whatsoever things are true, whatsoever things are honest, whatsoever things are just, whatsoever things are pure, whatsoever things are lovely, whatsoever things are of good report; if there be any virtue, and if there be any praise, think on these things." Philippians 4:8** Liberty comes from God. Bondage comes from Satan. Even though that spirit of bondage is trying to come upon the United States, God can hold back the darkness. We need to pray and seek face of God—not that Obama will be struck by lightning or drones fall out of sky—that people will be turned to God. Matthew 3:10, **"And now also the axe is laid unto the root of the trees: therefore every tree which bringeth not forth good fruit is hewn down, and cast into the fire."** The drones, NSA spying, N.W.O., political corruption: all of that is just fruit, the result of the devil carrying out his plan. **"When**

the righteous are in authority, the people rejoice: but when the wicked beareth rule, the people mourn." Proverbs 29:2. Satan is the root cause of every encroachment upon our liberty. When we wake up and see the situation the way God does, we can lay the axe "to the root of the tree;" we can get to the source of the problem.

We have been born for such a time as this! *America can come back to the Lord!* But it will not happen through a political process. We should have learned our lesson with President Bush. He was a Republican president who had a Republican majority in both the Senate and House of Representatives, but did he do anything about abortion? No! Republicans and Democrats, presidents and congressional leaders are all just politicians, they are not our Savior. The Lord Jesus Christ is our Savior. The only thing that can save the USA is the Spirit of the Living God sweeping across the land in Revival.

Israel was in deep sin, even openly sacrificing children to false Gods when Jeremiah wrote these words: **"For thus saith the Lord, That after seventy years be accomplished at Babylon I will visit you, and perform my good word toward you, in causing you to return to this place." Jeremiah 29:10.** America has been going thru a time of disobedience similar to the nation of Israel in Jeremiah's day. But God was not finished with Israel, for He said, "I will visit and cause you to return to this place." God is not finished with the United States of America either. He wants to "turn away" our captivity

Jeremiah 29:11-14, "For I know the thoughts that I think toward you, saith the Lord, thoughts of peace, and not of evil, to give you an expected end. Then shall ye call upon me, and ye shall go and pray unto me, and I will hearken

163

unto you. And ye shall seek me, and find me, when ye shall search for me with all your heart. And I will be found of you, saith the Lord: and **I will turn away your captivity**, and I will gather you from all the nations, and from all the places whither I have driven you, saith the Lord; and I will bring you again into the place whence I caused you to be carried away captive."** Those verses are a message for us, a Now Word, a Rhema Word. God wants to bless us, not to curse us. His Will is for all of us to come to the saving knowledge of Jesus Christ. Hell was created for Satan and his fallen angels, not for humanity. God wants us to be saved!

True Christians are supposed to have the mind of Christ. (**Philippians 2:5, "Let this mind be in you, which was also in Christ Jesus"** and I Corinthians 2:16, **"For who hath known the mind of the Lord, that he may instruct him? But we have the mind of Christ."**) We are supposed to think the thoughts of Christ, and Jesus came to do the will of the Father. God does not want to destroy people. It is Satan who comes to steal, kill, destroy and divide people. And he will continue to do so until the tribulation period, when he will try to unite humanity under the One World Government of the anti-Christ. But that time has not yet come, and right now Satan is still trying to create confusion and chaos. We, this generation, are called by God to take a stand against the darkness and evil. We are to be salt and light. If salt looses savor it is thrown onto a dung hill, according to Jesus' illustration, it is worthless. **"Salt is good: but if the salt have lost his savour, wherewith shall it be seasoned? It is neither fit for the land, nor yet for the dunghill; but men cast it out. He that hath ears to hear, let him hear." Luke 14:34-35.**

God sees the USA as a beacon of His Hope to the world. The people of the world see the United States as a beacon of hope as well. Outside the American embassy in the Philippines, there are literally hundreds of people lined up every day trying to come to United States. (There are not throngs of people outside of other countries' embassies wanting to get in to those nations.) I started two Filipino churches in States, and observed that these new immigrants had faced many social and cultural barriers to Evangelical Christianity in their home country. They had come to the United States from a society in which the collective drags people down to the lowest common denominator. But when these Filipino people got to the United States, away from their relatives and free of the spiritual bondage in their old country, one of the very first things that happen is they get Saved. I've seen it hundreds of times. This is what America is all about.

John 10 :10, "The thief cometh not, but for to steal, and to kill, and to destroy: I am come that they might have life, and that they might have it more abundantly." Life abundantly! God wants us to be blessed going in blessed going out, blessed in city and blessed in the country. (**Deuteronomy28:6, "Blessed shalt thou be when thou comest in, and blessed shalt thou be when thou goest out." Deuteronomy 28:3, "Blessed shalt thou be in the city, and blessed shalt thou be in the field."**) Hebrews says we have a better covenant. (**Hebrews 8:6b. "He is the mediator of a better covenant, which was established upon better promises."**) We are redeemed from curse of the law! (**Galatians 3:13, "Christ hath redeemed us from the curse of the law, being made a curse for us: for it is written, Cursed is every one that hangeth on a tree"**) We are the head not the tail! (**Deuteronomy 28:13, "And the**

Lord shall make thee the head, and not the tail; and thou shalt be above only, and thou shalt not be beneath; if that thou hearken unto the commandments of the Lord thy God, which I command thee this day, to observe and to do them") Blessed and highly favored! Favor isn't fair. God blesses his children. We do things for our own children that we would not do for other peoples' children because they belong to us. We give our children the best life we can, we don't kill our children, we love them. God is a *better* parent than we are. Jesus said, **"you being evil know how to give good gifts to your children, how much more shall your Father which is in heaven give good things to them that ask him?" (Matthew 7:11)**

Several years ago, the Lord showed me a vision of President Obama. In the vision, the White House and President Obama were in the palm of God's hand. I believe that God can use Barak Obama, because I saw him in God's hand. Even if his heart is not perfect toward God, that does not limit God's ability to use him for His glory. There are many examples in the Bible of God using pagan kings to accomplish His will. We should be praying for him to repent and turn to God because our job is to pray for His Mercy on people.

We reap what we sow. God help us to sow mercy! **"Righteousness exalteth a nation: but sin is a reproach to any people." Proverbs 14:34.** Righteousness from the Church, from the people of God is what America needs. Those who believe not are condemned already according to **John 3:18, "He that believeth on him is not condemned: but he that believeth not is condemned already, because he hath not believed in the name of the only begotten Son of God."** But we want them to be saved, not condemned. The good news is we are not under the law. We have the Good News of Jesus Christ now! Jesus is saying, "Repent, turn to me, all who are weary, heavy laden and I'll give you rest. " I am convinced that it is God's will is for America to be what it was called to be.

We can see the Lord's view of the world, contrasted with our view of the world in **John 4:5-7, "Then cometh he to a city of Samaria, which is called Sychar, near to the parcel of ground that Jacob gave to his son Joseph.[6] Now Jacob's well was there. Jesus therefore, being wearied with his journey, sat thus on the well: and it was about the sixth hour.[7] There cometh a woman of Samaria to draw water: Jesus saith unto her, Give me to drink."**

The woman at the well saw Jesus as a Jew, and wondered why He would talk to her, a Samaritan. Moreover, in those days, men and women would not normally speak to one another. **John 4:11, "Then saith the woman of Samaria unto him, How is it that thou, being a Jew, askest drink of me, which am a woman of Samaria? for the Jews have no dealings with the Samaritans."** If you read the stories of the kings after the death of Solomon, you will see that Samaria, to stop their people from going up to Jerusalem, had put a tabernacle on their own mountain and eventually fell into idolatry. Samaria in the Old Testament *never* had a single period of revival in the rest of their history. God had chosen Jerusalem for His temple and the tribe of Judah to bring forth the Messiah (Jesus). Judah considered Samaria to be unholy, unrighteousness, and backslidden, in the same way we Americans feel about certain parts of our country that have so openly turned away from God and embraced sin.

John 4:16-19, "Jesus saith unto her, Go, call thy husband, and come hither.[17]** The woman answered and said, I have no husband. Jesus said unto her, Thou hast well said, I have no husband:**[18]** For thou hast had five husbands; and he whom thou now hast is not thy husband: in that saidst thou truly.**[19]** The woman saith unto him, Sir, I perceive that thou art a prophet."**

This woman was at the well at noon. (6th hour of the day was noon) because she was an outcast. In a hot desert climate, people draw water in the early morning or just at dusk, not in the heat of the day. Her being at the well at noon, tells us, she was an outcast. But she was there at noon to avoid the other women of the town because of her many marriages and adultery. Obviously the disciples were religious people, yet they saw a Samaritan, a woman, and a harlot. To them she was a second class citizen on three counts!

The world today would think a woman with five divorces is perfectly okay. It is the self righteous (religious, church goers) who would condemn her. But Revival is neither about the world, nor is about the false vision of God's people. The disciples are a perfect example of the attitude of the modern church toward the sinful world. **John 4:27, "And upon this came his disciples, and marvelled that he talked with the woman: yet no man said, What seekest thou? or, Why talkest thou with her"** When the disciples saw the woman, they wondered why was Jesus was even talking to her. But, Jesus saw an Evangelist!

John 4:28-30, "The woman then left her water pot, and went her way into the city, and saith to the men,[29]** Come, see a man, which told me all things that ever I did: is not**

this the Christ?[30] **Then they went out of the city, and came unto him."** He revealed to her that He was the Messiah and sent her to tell the Good News! This is just what He wants all of us to do! Religion twists the Word to say divorced people are under sin forever. God says, we are free in the Son, and all Christians can proclaim the Good News!

The disciples, like the Church, were worried about satisfying the flesh, tending to temporal matters, getting the fellow church members together for a pot luck dinner. But our Lord said, I HAVE MEAT TO EAT YOU DO NOT KNOW ABOUT. **John 4:31-34, "In the mean while his disciples prayed him, saying, Master, eat.[32] But he said unto them, I have meat to eat that ye know not of.[33] Therefore said the disciples one to another, Hath any man brought him ought to eat?[34] Jesus saith unto them, My meat is to do the will of him that sent me, and to finish his work."**

Jesus often spoke in parables which have multiple meanings, a natural meaning and spiritual meaning which can only be seen through spiritual eyes and heard through spiritual ears. Here in John 4, he began to speak to His disciples about the harvest. **John 4:35-38,"Say not ye, There are yet four months, and then cometh harvest? behold, I say unto you, Lift up your eyes, and look on the fields; for they are white already to harvest.[36] And he that reapeth receiveth wages, and gathereth fruit unto life eternal: that both he that soweth and he that reapeth may rejoice together.[37] And herein is that saying true, One soweth, and another reapeth.[38] I sent you to reap that whereon ye bestowed no labour: other men laboured, and ye are entered into their labours."** When Jesus said, "Don't say that there is still four months until the harvest" he was rebuking them because they could not see or believe that the Samaritans could receive the Gospel. The Lord Jesus does not have a narrow view of the harvest. He said, "The field is the WORLD!" **Matthew 13:38-39, "<u>The field is the world</u>; the good seed are the children of the kingdom; but the tares are the children of the wicked one;[39] The enemy that sowed them is the devil; the harvest is the end of the world; and the reapers are the angels."** The Harvest is ready NOW! It is the Laborers that are few.

Revival came to the town of Sychar that day because Jesus saw a Harvest and an Evangelist, instead of a lost cause and a harlot! May the Lord Jesus open our eyes that we might have our eyes lifted up to see the Harvest is plentiful and that we might go into the harvest!

As in the story of Jonah and the Whale, Jonah could not see how God would want to bring revival to Nineveh. They were an immoral people. They had been cruel to Israel. Yet God told Jonah to go there and preach that judgment was coming so that they would repent. The Lord told Jonah, that Nineveh did not know their right hand from their left, and they needed Him. God loved these wicked people and sent warning. There was a harvest there. Revival came to that generation and Nineveh was not destroyed for another 100 years.

Yes, America has fallen far and fast because we, the people of God, have not stood in the gap. The church has not followed the Holy Spirit-inspired wisdom of King Solomon in 2 Chronicles 7:14. to repent and call out to Him. (**2 Chronicles 7:14 "If my people, which are called by my name, shall humble themselves, and pray, and seek my face, and turn from their wicked ways; then will I hear from heaven, and will forgive**

their sin, and will heal their land.") But it is not too late! We can still repent, seek Him, and ask Him for revival and power to turn this all around! Is not Jesus the Lord of the harvest? Are we so cold-hearted that we desire to depart (be Raptured) and let the world, who do not know their right hand from their left, perish? God Forbid! Let the Church seek our Lord that He may arise and let His enemies be scattered! **Psalm 68:1 "Let God arise, let his enemies be scattered: let them also that hate him flee before him."** May we the Church be filled with the love of Christ and the power of the Holy Spirit so that we might abound in good works for the sake of the Gospel.

I want to close this book with a Word from the Lord, a final charge, given to me as I was writing this chapter: "Be fruitful, and multiply. Replenish the church with My Love. I will infuse you with My Love. My Love is a consuming fire! My love is furiously stirred for the lost! Tell the people I AM calling, 'COME HOME! THE WEDDING BANQUET IS READY!' "

Patrick Winfrey

CHARTS & GRAPHS

**"My people are destroyed for lack of knowl-
edge: because thou hast rejected knowledge,
I will also reject thee, that thou shalt be no
priest to me: seeing thou hast forgotten the
law of thy God, I will also forget thy children.
As they were increased, so they sinned
against me: therefore will I change their glory
into shame." Hosea 4:5-6**

A merica has gone from a time of most people in the country
knowing the Gospel to a time of darkness in the Spirit,
and in the world. Crime and lawlessness has gripped our culture.
Abortion has robbed an entire generation of life. Divorce has
left the family in disarray. And people have exited the church
doors in massive numbers. The decline in church attendance
has happened simultaneously with the decline in every other
aspect of the culture. **"So then faith cometh by hearing, and
hearing by the word of God." Romans 10:17**. The following
charts and graphs show visual evidence of that decline.

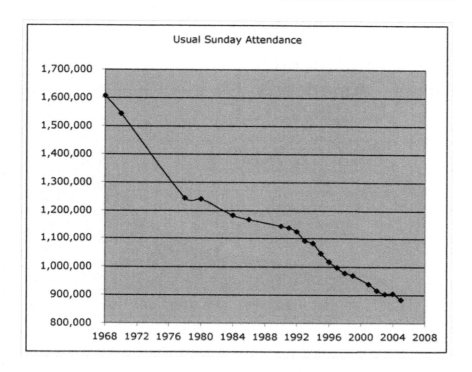

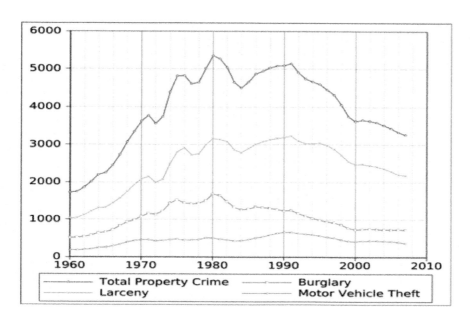

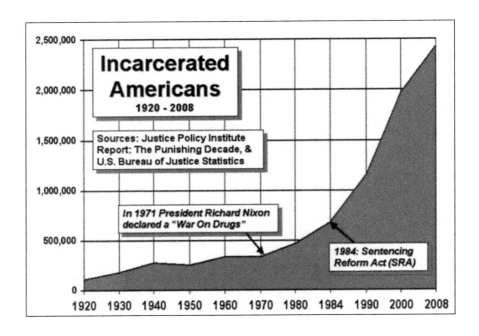

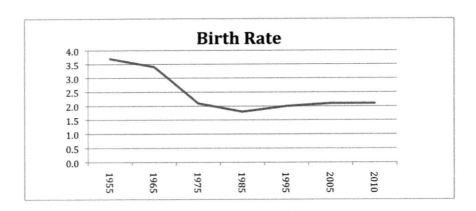

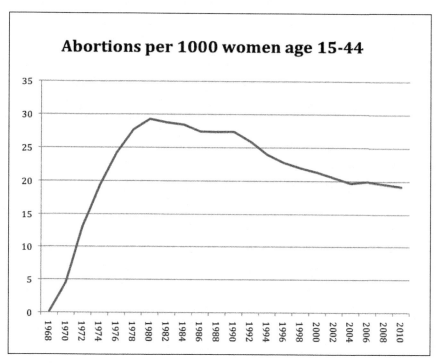

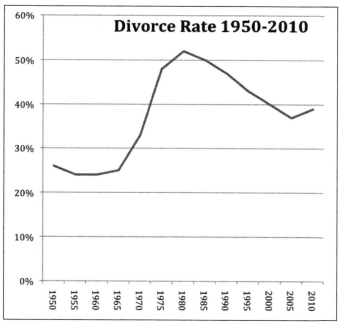

SUGGESTED READING ON THE SATANIC ROOTS OF THE NEW AGE MOVEMENT:

Helena Blavatsky–*The Divine Plan*

Alice A. Bailey–*The Plan*

Lucis Trust–*The Plan On Earth*

Albert Pike–*The Luciferian Age*

Aleister Crowley–*The Predicted New Era, The New Age, The Age Of Horus, The New Aeon, The Great Work, The World State*

Scottish Rite 33rd Degree Masonry–*The New Age*

St Germain–*The Aquarian Age*

Foster Gamble–*The Thrive Movement*

Theosophy–*The Quest, The Aquarian Age*

David Spangler–*The New Age*

George Bush Sr.–*1000 Points Of Light, Age of Freedom*

George Bush Sr.–*New World Order*

George W Bush–*Novous Ordo Seclurum "New Order of The Ages"*

Benjamin Creme–*The New Age, The Age of Maitreya "the Christ"*

David Icke–*The New Consciousness Shift, The 2012 the Awakening, Ascension*

Barbara Marx Hubbard–*Conscious Evolution, Awakening Power of Social Potential*

Terrence McKenn–*The 2012 Awakening*

David Wilcox–*Mayan 2012 Awakening, The New Golden Age*

Jacque Fresco–*The Venus Project*

Aldous Huxley–*Brave New World, The World State*

H. G Wells–*The New World Order*

> "No one may enter the New World Order unless he or she will make a pledge to worship Lucifer. No one will be allowed to enter the New Age unless he will take a Luciferian Initiation"–David Spangler, Director of Planetary Initiative, United Nations

Sources Cited:

1. Chapin, Henry and Denis Deneau. Citizen involvement in Public Policy-making: Access and the Policy-making Process. Ottawa, Canadian Council on Social Development, 1978. p. 33.

2. http://en.wikipedia.org/wiki/Mein_Kampf retrieved 19 June 2013.

3. Stock, Gregory (2002). *Redesigning Humans: Choosing our Genes, Changing our Future*. Mariner Books. ISBN 0-618-34083-1. OCLC 51756081.

4. Moore, Randy, The American Biology Teacher, Vol. 60, No. 8 (Oct., 1998), pp. 568-577

5. Crowley, Aleister (1989). *The Confessions of Aleister Crowley: An autohagiography*. London: Arkana. ISBN 978-0-14-019189-9.

6. http://www.christianpost.com/news/wicca-experts-encourage-christians-to-engage-america-s-fastest-growing-religion-34408/ retrieved 23June2013

7. Fensch, Thomas. *The FBI Files on Elvis Presley*, pp.15-17

8. Simons, David (2004). *Studio Stories—How the Great New York Records Were Made*. San Francisco: Backbeat Books.Cf. pp.168–169.

9. Simons, David (2004). *Studio Stories—How the Great New York Records Were Made*. San Francisco: Backbeat Books.Cf. ch.99, page 317

10. http://en.wikipedia.org/wiki/Rock_and_roll. retrieved 15 May2013

11. John Greenway, 'Jimmie Rodgers: A Folksong Catalyst', *The Journal of American Folklore*, Vol. 70, No. 277. (Jul-Sept 1957), pp. 231-234

12. http://en.wikipedia.org/wiki/Robert_Leroy_Johnson retrieved 9 April 2013

13. Mother Jones: *Fact-checking the Life and Death of Blues Man, Robert Johnson,* by Joe Kloc, 21 June 2010, retrieved 2 May 2013

14. Miller, 2000, pg 72

15. Geller, Larry "If I Can Dream", pg 139-141

16. Geller, pg 1599-160

17. White, Charles. The Life and Times of Little Richard: The Quasar of Rock". New York: Harmony, 1984

18. White, pg 41

19. *Little Richard, quoted in: quoted in Charles White, The Life and Times of Little Richard, Pt. 4, 1984*

20. Source:http://math.mercyhurst.edu/~griff/ sgtpepper/sgt. htmlretrieved 4May2013

21. Matus, Victorino (June 2004). "The Truth Behind "LSD"". The Weekly Standard

22. Source: Wikipedia® Melton, J. Gordon – Director Institute for the Study of American Religion. New Age Transformed, retrieved 29 April 2013

23. People Magazine, 8/22/88, pg 70

24. Paul McCartney interview on Larry King Live, CNN, 6/12/2001

25. YOKO ONO, The Playboy Interviews with John Lennon and Yoko Ono, Berkeley, 1982, p.106

26. Rolling Stone 8/11/1988, pg 51-52

27. Wikipedia.org/wiki/Never_Learn_Not_to_Love retrieved 9 April 2013

28. *Huffington Post via Life.com* CHARLES MANSON RANCHES first posted 9/6/09; updated 5/25/11, retrieved 18 April 2013

29. George-Warren 2001, p. 429: *Are You Experienced* certified double-platinum; Levy 2005, p. 34: Hendrix's "epochal debut"

30. Dave hunt, *America: The Sorcerer's New Apprentice,* Eugene OR: Harvest House, 1988 pp 230-240

31. Blake,William *The Marriage of Heaven and Hell.*

32. Riordan and Prochnicky "Break on Through: The Life & Death of Jim Morrison, 1988, pg 72

33. Riordan and Prochnicky, pg 23

34. Riordan and Prochnicky, pg 295-296

35. "March 5, 1969: Jim Morrison charged with lewd behavior at a Miami concert" http://www.history.com/this-day-in-history3/5?catId=4) retrieved 11 April 2013

36. Riordan & Prochnicky, pg 200

37. *Rolling Stone Magazine*, July 1999

38. *Rolling Stone Magazine*, cover Story "The Epic Life of Carlos Santana, March 15, 2000, p41

39. http://en.wikipedia.org/wiki/Rob_Halford retrieved 12 April 2013

40. *Faces,* November 1983, p.24

41. Bill Ward, BLACK SABBATH, cited in "Black Sabbath, an Oral History" p. 7

42. Media's Effect on Violence: A closer Look at Song Lyrics, Jul 30, 2007, retrieved 1 May 2013

43. http://en.wikipedia.org/wiki/The_Book_of_Abramelin retrieved 27 May 2013

44. Seay, David, "Stairway to Heaven" pg 249

45. http://www.reversespeech.com/stairway.htm, retrieved 12 April 2013

Sources Cited:

46. *Hit Parade* magazine, July 1985, pg 60

47. http://en.wikipedia.org/wiki/Richard_Ramirez, retrieved 13 April 2013

48. *Details for Men,* July 1991, pp. 100-101

49. *Rolling Stone*, MICHAEL JACKSON interview, 2/17/83

50. en.wikipedia.org/widi/The_Book_of_the_Law retrieved 27 May 2013

51. http://www.judiciaryreport.com/celebrities_who_suffered_tragedy_in_the_occult.htm retrieved 28May2013

52. *Reuters*, David Bowie/Ziggy Stardust, by Dan Fletcher, Friday July 10, 2009, retrieved 11 April 2013

53. Ibid, February 12, 1976, p. 83

54. Source: http://www.digitalspy.com/celebrity/...inside-me.html retrieved 20 April 2013

55. *Reuters*, Eminem/Slim Shady by Dan Fletcher, Friday, July 10, 2009, retrieved 11 April 2013

56. *People Magazine*, Beyonce, November 2008

57. http://en.wikipedia.org/wiki/Baphomet/image retrieved 18 May 2013

58. *The Black Flame*, Vol. 6., No. 1&2

59. *The Black Flame*, Vol. 6, numbers 1, Oct 1996, pg 37

60. Bloom, *Closing of the American Mind, 1987, pp. 73-74*

61. "Hip Hop: National Geographic World Music". Worldmusic. nationalgeographic.com. 2002-10-17. Retrieved 5 May 2013

62. "Nicki Minaj Makes History With Seven Billboard Hot 100 Songs". *MTV News*. October 8, 2010. Retrieved 5 May 2013

63. Lamb, Yvonne Shinhoster (2005-10-13). "C. Delores Tucker Dies at 78; Rights and Anti-Rap Activist". *The Washington Post*. pp. B4. Retrieved 5 May 2013.

64. aloftyexistence.wordpress.com/2011/06/20/rap-rock-vio-lence/retreived 1May2013

65. Pareles. John. Distributor Withdraws Rap Album Over Lyrics. New York Times. 28 August 1990. Retrieved 1 May 2013

66. http://www.wnd.com/2009/04/95038/.retrieved 18June2013

67. http://www.infowars.com/homeland-security-re-port-lists-liberty-lovers-as-terrorists/ retrieved 19 June 2013

68. http://en.wikipedia.org/wiki/Brave_new_world retrieved 5July2013

69. http://www.henrymakow.com/hg_wells_prophet_of_the_new_wo.html#sthash.L7eUj0FY.dpuf retrieved 7July 2013

70. http://www.henrymakow.com/hg_wells_prophet_of_the_new_wo.html 7 July 2013

71. Williamson, Lola (2010). *Transcendent in America: Hindu-Inspired Meditation Movements (HIMM) as New Religion.* New York, NY: New York University Press. p. 31. ISBN 978-0-8147-9449-4.

72. http://www.techhive.com/article/189844/Federal Judge Orders_School_Stop_Webcam_Spying_on_Students_at_Home.html retrieved 26June2013

73. http://www.dslserviceproviders.org/blog/10-attempts-to-provide-internet-access-to-third-world-countries/ retrieved 26 June 2013.

74. http://www.dailymail.co.uk/sciencetech/article-2344398/Google-futurist-claims-uploading-entire-MINDS-computers-2045-bodies-replaced-machines-90-years.html#ixzz2XNbRXoxh retrieved 19 June 2013

75. FBI, Uniform Crime Reports website, retrieved 4/9/2013

76. http://www.city-data.com/forum/politics-other-controversies/791894-1950s-vs-today-wages-dollar-compare-4.html#ixzz2U9Gc2EyP retrieved 22May2013

77. http://www.thefiscaltimes.com/Articles/2012/04/05/How-Well-Can-You-Live-on-Minimum-Wage.aspx#page1#ixzz2U7ZqQ0NB retrieved 8May2013

78. http://www.bls.gov/opub/uscs/1950.pdf retrieved 8May2013

79. Gloria Steinem:How the CIA UsedFeminism to Destabilize Society *By Henry Makow Ph.D.* | March 18,2002 retrieved 8 May2013

80. The Margaret Sanger Papers. Sophia Smith Collection, Smith College, Northampton, Mass. 1995. Retrieved 2013-06-19.

81. Engelman, Peter C. (2011), *A History of the Birth Control Movement in America*, ABC-CLIO, <u>ISBN 978-0-313-36509-6</u>

82. http://www.modernmom.com/article/when-did-the-birth-control-pill-become-available? By Michelle Powell-Smith, March 30, 2010, retrieved 10 June 2013

83. <u>http://en.wikipedia.org/wiki/Griswold_v._Connecticut retreived 14 June 2013</u>

84. <u>http://www.epm.org/resources/1999/Nov/02/birth-control-pill-abortifacient-and-contraceptive retrieved 11 June 2013</u>

85. <u>http://www.hipplanet.com/books/atoz/sex.htm retrieved 17 June 2013</u>

86. <u>http://postabortionsyndrome.org/retrieved 21June2013</u>

87. <u>http://images</u> Historical Look at Women's Participation Rates In the Labor force retrieved 18 June 2013.

88. <u>http://divorce.lovetoknow.com/Historical_Divorce_Rate_Statistics retrieved 17 June 2013</u>

89. June 2013 Church of God *Evangel,* Volume 103, issue 6, "Babies before Marriage"

90. http://www.sciencedaily.com/
releases/2008/03/080312172614.htm retrieved
21June2013

91. http://www.aglp.org/gap/1_history/ retrieved
18 June 2013

92. http://www.apa.org/topics/sexuality/transgender.pdf
retrieved 25June2013

93. http://godfatherpolitics.com/11028/elementa-
ry-school-hosts-cross-dressing-day-for-1st-and-2nd-grad-
ers/#ixzz2Wpktvddn retrieved 1June2013

94. http://www.timesfreepress.com/news/2013/jun/01/
lutheran-assembly-elects-first-openly-gay-bishop/
retrieved 6June2013

95. http://www.timesfreepress.com/news/2013/jun/01/
lutheran-assembly-elects-first-openly-gay-bishop/
retrieved 6June2013

96. http://www.breitbart.com/Big-Hollywood/2013/05/28/
Children-network-transsexual-superhero retrieved
2 June 2013

97. http://cnsnews.com/news/article/hhs-website-girls-10-16-
informs-youth-about-birth-control-gay-sex-mutual-mas-
turbation#sthash.NJ3IVGvz.dpuf retrieved 3June2013

98. http://www.dailymail.co.uk/news/article-2334948/Tumblr-
post-gay-teens-voted-high-schools-cutest-couple-shared-
100-000-times-just-24-hours.html#ixzz2WpnNxlMK
retrieved 4June2013

99. http://www.dailymail.co.uk/news/article-2334652/29-year-old-teacher-arrested-allegedly-having-sex-16-year-old-female-student-mentoring.html retrieved 19June2013

100. http://www.dailymail.co.uk/news/article-2334652/29-year-old-teacher-arrested-allegedly-having-sex-16-year-old-female-student-mentoring.html retrieved 19June2013

101. http://news.yahoo.com/m-f-outdated-ids-worry-trans-gender-people-162953086.html retrieved 18June2013

102. Cameron, Playfair, Wellu, "The Longevity Of Homosexuals: Before and After the AIDS Epidemic, "Omega Journal of Death and Dying" 1994

103. Encyclopædia Britannica Online. http://www.britannica.com/eb/article-9037772 Retrieved 7June2013

104. Sandys, John Edwin (1910). *A companion to Latin studies*. Chicago: University of Chicago Press. pp. 811–812.

105. DeHammel, Christopher, The Book: a History of the Bible, 2001

106. I. S. Robinson, "Pope Gregory VII, the Princes and the Pactum 1077–1080' *The English Historical Review* 94 No. 373 (October 1979):721–756) p. 725.

107. Carney, Jo Eldridge (2000). *Renaissance and Reformation, 1500–1620: a*. Greenwood Publishing Group. ISBN 0-313-30574-9.

108. Ludwig Ott, Verlag Herder, Freibury, 1952; published in English as *Fundamentals of Catholic Dogma*, Ludwig Ott, translated by Dr. Patrick Lynch and edited by James Canon Bastible, D.D.,The Mercier Press, Limited, May, 1955.

109. John Paul II, <u>Message to the Pontifical Academy of Sciences on Evolution</u>; the speech was made in French–for a dispute over whether the correct English translation of *"la theorie de l'evolution plus qu'une hypothese"* is "more than a hypothesis" or "more than one hypothesis", see <u>Eugenie Scott, NCSE online version</u> of *Creationists and the Pope's Statement*, which originally appeared in *The Quarterly Review of Biology*, 72.4, December 1997

110. John Paul II, <u>Message to the Pontifical Academy of Sciences on Evolution</u>; the speech was made in French–for a dispute over whether the correct English translation of *"la theorie de l'evolution plus qu'une hypothese"* is "more than a hypothesis" or "more than one hypothesis", see <u>Eugenie Scott, NCSE online version</u> of *Creationists and the Pope's Statement*, which originally appeared in *The Quarterly Review of Biology*, 72.4, December 1997

111. <u>http://blog.al.com/forthelove/2008/05/the_extraterrestrial_is_my_bro.html retrieved 9July2013</u>

112. Jutta Leonhardt *Jewish worship in Philo of Alexandria* Page 270–2001

113. http://www.christianitytoday.com/ch/131christians/
     denominationalfounders/wesley.html?start=
     1retrieved 8July2013

114. Hurst, J. F. (2003). *John Wesley the Methodist.*
     Kessinger Publishing. pp. 102–103. ISBN
     0-7661-5446-7

115. Sydney E. Armstrong, *A Religious History of the
     American People.* (1972) p. 263

116. http://www.nytimes.com/1989/06/20/nyregion/
     new-methodist-hymnal-is-shorn-of-stereotypes.html
     retrieved 8July2013

117. Sowler, Sidney D.; Marjorie H. Royle (2005-06-27).
     "Worshiping into God's Future: Summaries and
     Strategies 2005" (PDF). ucc.org. Archived from the
     original on 2006-12-26. Retrieved 8 July 2013.

118. http://articles.chicagotribune.com/2003-11-03/
     news/0311030218_1_gay-bishop-consecration-nation-
     al-church retrieved 9July 2013

119. http://www.cnn.com/2010/US/05/15/episcopal.lesbian.
     bishop/index.html?_s=PM:US retrieved 9July2013

120. http://www.pinknews.co.uk/2013/01/10/anglican-nige-
     rian-church-threatens-to-split-from-church-of-england-
     over-gay-bishops-row/ retrieved 8July2013

121. http://www.infobarrel.com/Lutheran_
     Marriage#H5cAPoUCwd5vZpla.99 retrieved 8July2013

122. http://www.ocregister.com/articles/muslims-341669-warren-saddleback.html retrieved 9July2013

123. http://www.nowtheendbegins.com/blog/?p=5441 retrieved 8July2013

124. http://www.prophecynewswatch.com/2012/February01/0152.html retrieved 9July2013

125. http://www.religioustolerance.org/virgin_b7.htm retrieved 9July2013

126. http://www.churchleaders.com/pastors/pastor-articles/139575-7-startling-facts-an-up-close-look-at-church-attendance-in-america.html retrieved 12July2013

ABOUT THE AUTHOR

Matthew Patrick Winfrey has been in the ministry since 2001, starting as an associate pastor in an evangelical church. In 2002, the Lord led him to begin working with Filipino immigrants in the United States. He planted three Filipino churches in the Triad region of North Carolina, and graduating from Global University in Springfield, MO in 2005, with a BA in Missions, began short-term mission work in the Philippines. He has been a full-time missionary in the Philippines since August, 2007, where he has planted many churches and established a Bible School in addition to conducting revivals, evangelistic crusades, Pastor's conferences on the End Times, and medical missions.

With the death of his five year old step-son Joshua in August 2012, the Lord gave him the vision for a new ministry to enable little children to lead their families to the Lord. It is called "Joshua's Ministry". The focus and vision of this ministry is that, like the Joshua of the Bible, his Joshua will lead the Filipino people out of the desert of idol worship, into the Promise Land of the Kingdom of the Lord Jesus Christ.

The Holy Spirit has moved mightily through this situation. Within three months, the first orphanage was built, completed funded by God's Grace, and feeding programs were started through various churches that are now feeding and sharing the Gospel of our Lord Jesus Christ with 300-400 children per week. He and his wife, Jessa, along with a team of pastors and families, are now forcefully, and by faith, advancing the Kingdom for our Lord in the remote and largely never-before-evangelized areas of the Island of Mindanao, Philippines.

Now, with this book, the Lord, through Pastor Patrick Winfrey, is calling for revival, for a New Great Awakening to flood the USA with a tsunami of the God's glory!

PLEASE VISIT OUR WEBSITE
http://www.joshuasministry.com/

FEEL FREE TO EMAIL ME ALSO: neartochrist@aol.com

CPSIA information can be obtained at www.ICGtesting.com
Printed in the USA
BVOW11s0309260615

405894BV00012B/170/P

9 781628 391367